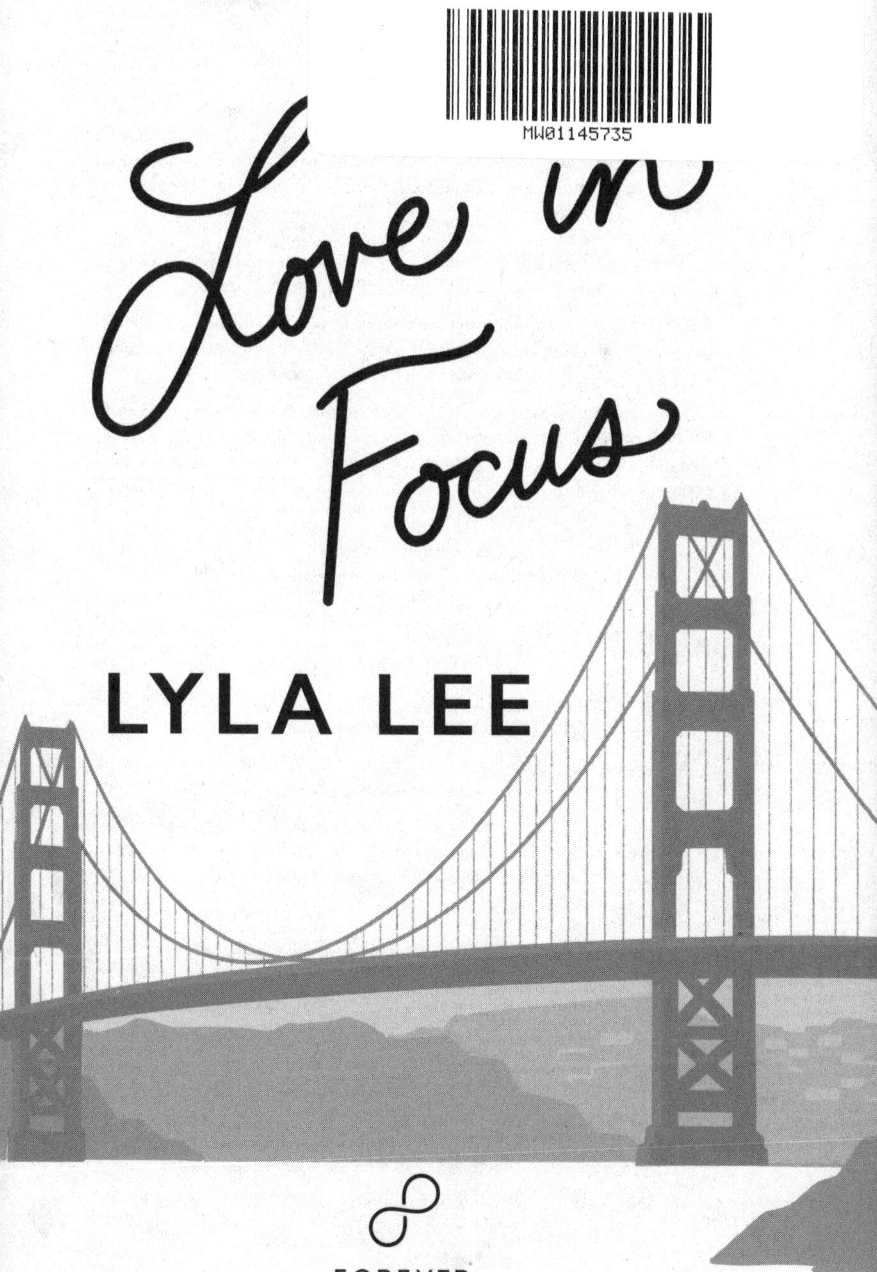

FOREVER
New York Boston

This book is a work of fiction. Names, characters, places, and incidents are the product of the author's imagination or are used fictitiously. Any resemblance to actual events, locales, or persons, living or dead, is coincidental.

Forever
Hachette Book Group
1290 Avenue of the Americas, New York, NY 10104
read-forever.com
@readforeverpub

First Edition: May 2025

Forever is an imprint of Grand Central Publishing. The Forever name and logo are registered trademarks of Hachette Book Group, Inc.

The publisher is not responsible for websites (or their content) that are not owned by the publisher.

Forever books may be purchased in bulk for business, educational, or promotional use. For information, please contact your local bookseller or the Hachette Book Group Special Markets Department at special.markets@hbgusa.com.

Print book interior design by Taylor Navis

Library of Congress Cataloging-in-Publication Data

Names: Lee, Lyla, author.
Title: Love in focus / Lyla Lee.
Description: First edition. | New York : Forever, 2025.
Identifiers: LCCN 2024058642 | ISBN 9781538767559 (trade paperback) | ISBN 9781538767566 (ebook)
Subjects: LCGFT: Romance fiction. | Queer fiction. | Novels.
Classification: LCC PS3612.E2253 L68 2025 | DDC 813/.6—dc23/eng/20241212
LC record available at https://lccn.loc.gov/2024058642

ISBNs: 9781538767559 (trade paperback), 9781538767566 (ebook)

Printed in the United States of America

CCR

10 9 8 7 6 5 4 3 2 1

For the women who love other women, and especially the ones who love everyone else, too

Gemma

True love doesn't exist. Or, at least, I'm not sure if it exists for me.

I know that's a grim statement coming from someone who writes for a romantic advice column. But I'm a realist. And I'm human, too. I'm not some wise, omniscient fairy godmother who doesn't have her own fucked-up love life to worry about.

In college, I fell deeply in love with my roommate, Celeste. I didn't even know I was bi until we met, and I loved her so much I was ready to come out to my very traditional Korean parents and possibly upend my entire life, just for her. But then the next year, Celeste not only dumped me through a text, but also moved back home to Seoul without any explanation whatsoever.

Then I met James, who I thought was the One. We dated seven years and got engaged. And even after all that, on one random, rainy day, he said he didn't love me anymore.

The beauty of being bi, I learned, is that you can get rejected by both women *and* men.

I press my forehead to the cold surface of the Muni train window. The rain's really coming down now, persistent and miserable. After living in sunny Southern California for the first twenty-two years of my life, I find San Francisco's wet season to be unbearable. Seven years of living here, and I still hate the cold rain and fog, which makes it seem colder than the fifty something degrees it really is.

In college, people called the journey home after a hookup the "walk of shame." Back then, getting caught doing the walk seemed like the worst thing ever, which, in hindsight, was pretty sad, because why should anyone be ashamed of having a sex life? But whatever shame I felt then is nothing compared to the utterly soul-crushing sense of failure I feel now on this train, on my way to crash on my friends' couch at age twenty-nine with a cardboard box filled with my stuff.

Half of my friends are engaged or married, while most of the rest are in long, committed relationships. Some even already have kids. Sure, a few are single, but a lot of those friends are uncoupled by choice. Meanwhile, I thought I'd be *married* by next year. Instead, here I am, newly single *and* without even my own place to call home. A rogue car spinning off the track as the others race past.

When I tearfully asked for—no, *demanded*—an explanation, James just frowned and apologized, saying he was sorry he didn't realize sooner he didn't want to marry me. And then, in an almost fugue state, I gave him back my ring, dumped all my favorite clothes and belongings in a box, and left. Because I didn't want to waste even another second with yet another person who clearly didn't want to be with me.

The train slows down to let people off at the next stop, and I close my eyes and try to look on the bright side. At least we're breaking up now, before we got married. I've heard enough horror stories through my relationship column to know it's much better to separate while we're engaged than to have to file for divorce later.

But as much as I try to be positive, when the train starts speeding up again, my thoughts spiral, and I think about how I *don't know* what went wrong. One moment, James and I were happy and talking about wedding venues, and then the next, I was putting my things in a box.

Maybe there's something wrong with me. Maybe I have a big MEANT TO BE FOREVER ALONE sign on my forehead that everyone can see except me. Whatever the reason, as much as I love love and made a whole career out of it, in my personal life, I give love my all, only for other people to decide they don't want to be with me. Well, romantically at least.

In the realm of friendship, though, I'm thankfully blessed. When I texted my best friends, Val and Kiara, about what happened, they immediately offered to let me crash at their apartment.

Come on over, girl, Kiara had replied. There's always space on Clementine for you.

Clementine is the name of Kiara's atrociously orange sofa, the one she managed to acquire in college for only five dollars. The legend goes that she bought the couch as a joke but never had the heart to get rid of it afterward. I've sat on it whenever I came over, and it seemed comfy enough. And apparently people sleep on it all the time whenever they have guests from out of town, so hopefully it'll be fine.

Thankfully, the rain stops by the time I get off the train and walk to the apartment with my box. The Inner Sunset, my friends' neighborhood, is on the opposite side of the city from where I lived with James, but it's still much closer than Irvine, in Southern California, where my parents are.

I've been to Kiara and Val's place plenty of times before, enough to know where to turn and which hill to climb. But I've never been here at night. Compared to the perpetually loud streets and brightly lit high-rises of my old neighborhood, my friends' street is dimly lit and quiet. Aside from the fleeting headlights of passing cars, the only sources of light are the streetlamps that dot the sidewalk and the occasionally uncovered windows of people's homes. After living near the hustle and bustle of the Financial District and Chinatown, I find the sudden silence jarring.

"Hey!" Kiara waves at me from where she's standing in the doorway to her building. She's holding the door open, and light filters out from the hall, casting a warm, faint glow on her pink braids and brown skin. When she sees my face, her expression softens, and she approaches me with her arms outstretched.

"Come here, baby," she says.

Tears erupt from the corners of my eyes as we hug. During the train ride, I naively thought I was done crying.

But now that I'm in the refuge of Kiara's arms, uncontrollable sobs rack my body. Waves of grief hit me one after another, each one leaving me emptier than the last.

"You're okay," Kiara says, gently patting my back. "Good riddance to him! He's a complete mess. I still can't believe he couldn't even give you a straight answer for why he's breaking up with you."

Val steps forward from behind Kiara to join our group hug. A direct contrast to Kiara's cute white blouse and pink skirt, Val's in a black turtleneck, khaki pants, and combat boots that, along with her fade haircut, make her look like she's about to report to basic training. They can't be more different, and yet they give off the same loving energy, incredibly in sync with each other in a way that only the luckiest couples are.

"You're all right, kid," Val says. "James was only dragging you down. There are lots of other men *and* women out there for you. Or even nonbinary folk! The world is your oyster."

I know her well enough to get that she's channeling her suburban white stepdad, Bill, to try to make me laugh. It's a bit she likes to do sometimes, since the phrases he commonly uses sound ridiculous coming from a petite, Mexican butch like her. And I'd be cackling, too, if I didn't feel so hollowed out inside.

Kiara pulls away and says, "Okay, so…we should go back inside before our neighbor throws a shoe at us."

I blink away tears. "Is that a real problem you guys have had?"

"Yeah... they hate us. Not everyone appreciates our spontaneous EDM parties."

"Why pay to rave when you can have a rave for free at home?" Val adds with a shrug. "Besides, I like not having to leave the apartment or deal with lots of people."

A small laugh finally escapes my mouth. Even though Kiara and Val are very different, they're still two peas in the same chaotic, but good, pod.

Val grabs one side of my box and tries to lift it up. "Geez!" she hisses. "How did you bring this heavy thing across the city? And walk up and down the hills?"

Kiara grabs the other side, while I hold the middle.

I shrug. "Just pure stubbornness I guess."

"Well, you don't have to go through everything alone anymore," Kiara says. "You're stuck with us now. For better or worse."

Quietly laughing, we carry the box up the stairs.

The first Monday after the breakup is even more excruciating than I thought it would be. For the most part, I love working for *Horizon Magazine*, one of the only surviving regional magazines in the San Francisco Bay Area, but even that feels like a big middle finger from life when I run into James on the elevator.

Yes, my ex is also my coworker. And yes, I've read the million think pieces about how you should never date someone from work. I've *written* some of them.

But in my defense, I met James in college during my senior year, so it's not like we started out as an office romance. Since we were two job-searching seniors, we dated casually at first. After what happened with Celeste, I was in no rush to get into another relationship. But when we were both hired by the same magazine fresh out of college, it seemed like destiny. And things got serious fast, especially after James's very well-off parents bought us a condo in San Francisco and we moved in together, four months after we met.

In retrospect, what James and I did was ill-advised. But back then, everything was so *fun* and exciting. We spent most of our twenties exploring every inch of the Bay Area together when we weren't at work, sometimes even *for* work, since I had to constantly visit new places for my articles. A good chunk of the memories I made since moving to the area, like eating clam chowder for the first time at Fisherman's Wharf or renting a convertible to drive down to Santa Cruz, were with James.

But today, James gets on the elevator, not even saying hi or otherwise acknowledging that I exist. It's so obvious from his unnaturally stiff posture that he's actively trying to avoid eye contact with me as we make our way up to where our office is on the fifth floor.

While he stares at the elevator buttons like it's his first time seeing them, I scrutinize his face, searching for red eyes, new wrinkle lines, or any other telltale sign that he's as fucked up about our breakup as I am. Or some clue as to why he decided to call off our engagement in the first place.

But every brown curl on his head is perfectly tousled, and his blue eyes look sharper than ever. If anything, he looks more well rested than usual. *Son of a bitch.*

By the time the elevator doors open again and we walk to our respective desks, I'm channeling my inner Lady Gaga. *Your career will never wake up and tell you it doesn't love you anymore. Your career will never wake up*... I repeat the mantra over and over in my head. Forget James. Forget *everyone.* I don't need to be in a relationship to win at life. In fact, historically, romantic relationships have only brought me down.

Single, powerful, beautiful. I repeat another mantra I once came up with for a newly divorced woman who asked for advice on the column. *I'm single, powerful, and beautiful.*

Pushing away all thoughts of James from my head, I focus on work until my lunch break.

My favorite time of the workday is lunch, since it was the only time my friends and I could regularly see each other during the week before I started living with them. With only twenty employees, *Horizon* is a pretty small magazine owned by Citrine, a larger, out-of-state parent company. But Val works in IT and Kiara in design, and our jobs keep us all busy. If it weren't for the icebreakers at a company-wide mixer seven years ago where we discovered we were obsessed with the same music artists, we might never have become friends in the first place.

"How are you holding up?" Kiara asks when we meet in front of the café on the first floor. Since Kiara and Val had to run some errands on their way to work this morning, we barely had time to say "hi" before they left.

"Well, I had an awkward run-in with James at the elevator," I reply. "He pretended I was invisible."

Kiara and Val groan.

"Maybe we could get him fired," Val jokes. "Want me to log in to his computer and see if he's been watching porn during work hours?"

Kiara giggles. "Oh God, I hope he hasn't."

"Same," I say. I don't *think* James would watch porn at work. But this past weekend taught me I don't know anything about him.

How can someone randomly decide they don't love you after seven years? Just like that?

A fresh burst of pain hits my chest, and for a split second, it's hard for me to breathe. If James and I fought a lot or if there was any noticeable tension between us, I might have been less blindsided. But besides a couple of minor disagreements here and there, which we quickly resolved with a joke or a laugh, I can't remember if we ever actually fought. Maybe that had been our problem, in the end. After all, *some* conflict is healthy. But I never thought that deeply about James's and my *lack* of conflict until the sudden death of our relationship.

I need a distraction. Fast. Hoping they won't notice the tears forming in the corners of my eyes, I steer my friends toward the line for food.

"I'm starving," I say. "Let's go eat. Can we talk about something other than James?"

Kiara's face pinches, like she can tell I'm not okay but she's trying her best not to say anything.

"Yup, sure thing," she says as we get in line. "Have you heard from Evelyn about the new project we're doing for Valentine's Day yet? The 'Modern Love in Focus' one? The freelance photographer they hired is *so* hot! I heard you're attached to conduct the interviews and write the text."

I'm always so deeply buried in emails on Mondays that I'm not surprised I haven't even heard of this project yet. But it sounds like the kind of ambitious work that Evelyn, our executive editor, would sign me up for. She's always been pushing me to do bigger and better things every year, even though I'm mostly content just writing local lifestyle stories and contributing to Dear Karl, *Horizon*'s romantic advice column that's named after the San Francisco fog.

Information about the project is probably in my inbox somewhere. I'll have to get to it after lunch.

"That sounds cool!" I say. "I haven't read that email yet. Do you remember the name of the photographer?"

"I forgot her name, and I don't think I'm supposed to share it anyway because she's not one hundred percent confirmed yet," Kiara says sheepishly. "But I remember seeing from her bio that she went to UCLA like you. And like I said, she's pretty. She looks like a model herself!"

I frown. My college ex, Celeste, was a photographer, but so were countless other women who went to my alma mater. I shake my head, like doing so will get rid of my thoughts of her.

Val raises her eyebrows. "Man, the way you're talking about her, I guess I should consider myself lucky that you're not into other femmes."

Kiara giggles, giving Val's arm a squeeze. "Oh, stop! And even if I were into both femmes *and* mascs, you know you're irreplaceable to me. There's no one else in the entire universe I'd rather date than you."

"I'm kidding," Val says, giving her a peck on the cheek. "Same here."

Suddenly feeling very *painfully* single, I stare up at the overhead menu.

Since I'm not in my early twenties anymore, I usually try to choose the healthier options, like the salads or veggie wraps. But today, I'm famished. And I need a little pick-me-up. My stomach is already growling from the rich smells of sweetly marinated beef permeating the air, so I decide on the Texas barbecue sandwich.

"Didn't you say you dated a photographer in college once?" Val suddenly asks me then. "Your 'the one who got away'?"

Kiara gasps. "Ooh, yeah! The roommate who made you realize you're not straight, right?"

"Yup," I reply with a sigh. "But it's probably not her. She broke up with me and moved back to Seoul during the winter break of our senior year without telling me why."

"Damn," says Val. "How long were you guys together?"

"A little over a year," I reply. "From fall quarter of junior year to the winter break of senior."

I've tried my best to talk about Celeste very minimally with my friends over the last several years, since (1) it's painful, and (2) I could pretty much predict what they'd say about her. So I'm not surprised when Val replies with, "A little over a year... during *college*? Wow, you two were basically engaged, then! As far as sapphics go, anyway."

I sigh. "Yeah. We had all these plans of what we were going to do after graduation. And then she just... disappeared one day."

Kiara grasps my arm, a pitying look on her face.

I turn away, refocusing on the menu. "Anyway, our school has one of the best photography programs in the country, and I'm sure a lot of alumni stay in state afterward, so it could be anyone, really."

"For your sake, I hope the photographer they hired is gay," Val remarks. "Like, even if she's not your ex. You deserve a sexy rebound."

I snort. "I'm not looking to date anyone anytime soon." The guy in front of me finishes ordering, so I add, "Right now, the only hot thing making my heart flutter is a smoky barbecue sandwich."

Kiara and Val laugh, and I wink at them before placing an order for the true love of my life.

2

Gemma

My resolve to stay single and focus on myself lasts for two weeks, until I walk in on James making out with one of my coworkers in the printer room.

She's mostly covered by him, but even so, I recognize Daphne Smith right away because, with her five-foot-eight height and long golden locks, she's a total Greek goddess of a human being who looks like she could be on *Bachelor in Paradise*. James has her pushed up against the far side wall, in a corner that's out of the overhead security camera's field of view, a fact I know because *James and I* have made out before in that very spot.

My stomach drops, and I freeze from the sheer shock of it all. The three of us are alone in the small space, and James and Daphne would have totally noticed me walking in if they hadn't been so disgustingly all over each other. Thankfully, they both still have their clothes on, but from the noises they're making, they may as well be naked. Sultry moans escape from Daphne's mouth, while James sounds like a cross between a caveman and a porn star.

I try to remember if he always sounded like that. If he did, I must have gotten used to it in my seven years of dating him. Suddenly, I feel very, very sorry for Past Gemma. And not only because she just walked in on her ex.

Belatedly, I turn around, deciding to get the papers I printed later. But before I can leave the room, the door opens, revealing Shane, one of my other coworkers.

Fuck.

Three things happen, in quick succession.

"Oh hey, Gemma," Shane says. "Is the printer jammed—"

James yells, "Shit!"

"Oh God!" Shane cries out, covering his eyes.

James and Daphne jump apart, and I mentally scream.

"What the fuck, Gemma?" exclaims James. "Have you been watching us this entire time?"

I raise my eyebrows. So *now* he decides to acknowledge my existence. Trying my best to avoid his gaze, I peer back at Daphne, instead. Her face is flushed, and she's glaring at me with utter contempt in her eyes. I can't say I blame her. In this one horrible moment, my coworker, my ex, and my ex's new... *something* all stare at me, eyes wide with confusion and disbelief.

"Don't flatter yourself," I say, trying to ignore the heat burning up my cheeks. "I was just trying to get some printouts. Speaking of which, excuse me!"

Zeroing in on the printer like a horse with blinders, I

rush in, grab the still-warm papers from the tray, and dash out before anyone else can say anything. On the off chance that James will chase me down, I speed into the elevator and repeatedly hit close.

The doors mercifully shut without incident, and I press the button for the first floor. In the sudden quiet, I feel numb all over as I lean against the back wall of the elevator. The world spins, and when I look down at my hands, it takes me a moment to register that yes, those are *my* hands that have accidentally crumpled up the papers I needed for work.

I sigh. I'll have to reprint those later.

Part of me wants to report James and Daphne to HR, but I don't want to be *that* person. Plus, the last thing I want to do is deal with the investigations that'll inevitably ensue from it.

How did I see them? Well, that's a funny story…

I'd be worried about Shane exposing us all, but James, being James, probably has that department covered. Knowing him, he's probably bribing the poor—or lucky?—guy with front-row tickets to a 49ers game right now. Tickets that James will easily get, thanks to Mom and Dad.

A part of me can't believe I ever dated this man. And for so long, too. But then I remember all the adventures we had around the city. The countless nights we spent playing video games and binge-watching TV. All the unmet whispered promises of forever love and—okay, fine—good sex.

I'm trembling head to toe by the time the elevator doors

reopen. Instead of going back up to the fifth floor, I exit the elevator and walk to the café. Since it's around ten a.m., it's mostly empty except for a handful of people eating a pastry or grabbing coffee to take back up.

I sit at one of the high tables. And then, pressing my palms into my eyes, I let out a shuddering breath.

Seven years of thinking I've met my perfect person. Seven years of thinking I had it all figured it out. All culminating in an extremely awkward encounter in *the printer room*, where he's eagerly making out with another woman a couple of weeks after he upended my life.

I open up my phone and scroll up to a text that Kiara sent a few days ago with links to different dating apps. She's been encouraging me to go out and meet new people, telling me I should have some fun since I'm a "free woman" now. I previously said no, because I didn't think I was ready yet.

And I'm still definitely not ready to date or anything like that now. But after seeing James with Daphne today, I want to get drunk and meet a bunch of hot people. Ones that *don't* make weird caveman noises.

Thankfully, when I'm back at my desk, everyone's working again. I can't see James's face from where his desk is on the opposite side of the room, but I see him hunched over his computer. Daphne and Shane are also at their respective desks, typing away as if absolutely nothing happened twenty minutes ago. What a bizarre day.

I send the documents I need to the printer again, and, while waiting for everything to print, I download a few dating apps. But once they've finished loading, I can't bring myself to open a single one.

Dating apps are daunting, especially since I know most people my age have already been on and off them. Meanwhile, I haven't used any before now, to the extent that whenever someone writes into Dear Karl asking for advice on dating apps, I automatically forward the question to another writer who's used them before. I wasn't old enough to use them when they first became popular, and in college, I met people in person, like Celeste and James.

Given my track record, maybe I'm better off letting an app help me meet someone.

I end up leaving the office later than I intended to, mainly because I throw myself deep into work to avoid thinking about my own shit show of a romantic life. I'm still reading long email chains I'm cc'd on as I ride the train back to my friends' apartment.

Things seem to be progressing slower than expected, as they often do in this industry due to the usual concoction of staff shortages, declining funds, and bureaucracy, so I have no idea who the mysterious photographer Kiara mentioned is yet. I'm not even remotely delusional enough to hope that the photographer they pair me up with will like other women, like Val had jokingly hoped. But it'll be nice to meet and spend time with someone new, even just platonically. I love Val and Kiara, but after two weeks of living with them, I'm tired of third wheeling. Hopefully the photographer and I can at the very least bond over memories of our alma mater.

Even if she *does* happen to be queer, I'm not sure if I'll even have the bandwidth to start anything because the stakes, as they often are these days, are high. According to Evelyn's emails, if we don't generate enough clicks or print sales in the next quarter, there's a good possibility that our parent company will rebrand the magazine altogether to focus on more profitable sectors like tech or real estate. Evelyn hasn't explicitly said what'll happen to us local lifestyle writers if and when this kind of rebranding happens, but I can guess the outcome. And because I don't know anything about computers or houses, I'll be out of a job.

Since everyone—or at least, a decent amount of people—loves love, Evelyn is hoping a big project like "Modern Love in Focus" will catch a lot of attention and will generate the necessary numbers to save our section. And I hope so, too, because I love my job. And the last thing I need right now on top of all the other turmoil I already have going on in my life is unemployment.

Despite the pressure, I'm excited for this project. "Modern Love in Focus," as Evelyn pitched it, will feature interviews with San Franciscan couples of three different generations, starting from college students to senior citizens, about their various experiences with love. The printed magazine will have interview transcripts and gorgeous portraits of the subjects, while the digital edition will have video recordings of the interviews. It's a cute, dream-come-true project that's right up my alley. The biggest opportunity I've ever had at *Horizon*. I make a mental note to thank Evelyn for assigning it to me.

By the time I get off the train, I'm so stoked about the project that it doesn't even bother me that my own personal life is a mess right now. If anything, focusing on other people's love lives sounds like an excellent distraction from my own.

Val and Kiara's apartment has a mostly open-plan layout, so the front door directly leads into not only the kitchen, but also the living room and Val's office space area in the far-right corner. The only walled-off areas are the single bathroom and my friends' bedroom, so when I step through the front door, I make direct eye contact with Val, who looks up from her multiple computer monitors.

"Hey," she says. "Missed you at lunch today. Everything all right?"

I only then realize I'd been so determined to distract myself from what happened this morning that I'd totally skipped lunch. As if on cue, my stomach growls.

"Not really," I reply. "But I'll tell you the full story later."

"'Kay."

Val goes back to her game, leaving me to marvel at her current setup. My friend is playing a first-person shooter game on one screen while also watching what looks like *Jujutsu Kaisen*, an anime, on the other. A stack of pizza boxes is precariously perched on the side table next to her computer.

It's a miracle that Kiara hasn't murdered her yet. I look

around and don't see any signs that she came back to the apartment after work yet. She must be out getting dinner with some of her other friends today. Out of the three of us, Kiara is the social butterfly, having so many different friend groups that it's hard for me to keep track.

As I watch, Burrito, their ginger cat, gets ready to pounce on the boxes.

"Val," I say. "Burrito is—"

"Yikes, got him!" Val pauses her game to scoop the cat up into her arms, just as he tries to jump. "Oh no, you don't! Nice try, *bichito*."

Burrito, at five years old, is now a massive male cat. But when my friends first got him, he was "about the size of a burrito." Thus, the name.

"Plus, we read this article once about this cat named Burrito who got tragically eaten by a Florida man's pet python," Val also told me. "Kiara named our Burrito in honor of that Burrito, too. So that in this life, Burrito the Cat can live a long, happy life."

I personally love both reasons because they're *very* much Val and Kiara.

Val sets Burrito back down on the ground and says, "There's still some pizza left if you want some. I got carried away and ordered too much."

"Thanks." After gladly grabbing a slice of pepperoni, I sit on Clementine to eat. The excitement I felt on the train is gone now, and without the adrenaline, I feel disconnected from my body. I can barely taste anything. But my hands are visibly shaking from fatigue and hunger, and it feels like I have a gaping hole in my stomach. So I grab another piece.

When I finish eating, I gently nudge Burrito aside to grab my toiletries and pajamas from my box in the corner of the room.

Like many apartments in San Francisco, my friends' place is expensive yet tiny, and their closets were already full with their own stuff. So I got myself a new, dry box where I could temporarily store my things. Sure, living out of a literal box gets annoying sometimes, but I haven't found any real reason to complain yet, especially since my friends are letting me stay at their place rent-free. I tried paying them, but Kiara and Val wouldn't allow it.

"Collecting rent from someone who's already at rock bottom is what a predatory landlord does," Kiara had said. "And that's not who we are at all. Besides, you don't even have your own room! Just a couch. Save the money for the deposit at your new place. We already paid rent for the month of November anyway, so if you want to, you can pay us whatever you can manage next month, if you haven't found somewhere else to live by then."

I get in the shower and make the water as hot as I can without burning myself. Only then does some of the numbness go away. By the time I get into my pajamas, my entire body is flushed red from the heat, but in a way that actually feels nice.

I resolve to not tell my friends about today. At least, not yet. I only just started feeling normal again. I don't want to completely shatter when I try to tell them about what I saw at work. Everything's still so raw.

Instead, when Kiara comes back, I announce, "So I downloaded dating apps. I've decided to try casual dating."

"Yay!" Kiara exclaims, at the same time Val asks, "You *what*? And how's that going?"

"Oh, um, I haven't tried any of them yet." I'm taken aback, since I'd assumed both Kiara and Val wanted me to get out there and meet new people.

"Wait, I thought you wanted me to date around," I say to Val. "Since you said that thing about the hot photographer."

"I do, but I was talking more in terms of in-person hookups. *Dating apps*... however." She winces. "Let's just say you're in for a wild ride."

I don't know what she means until I finish making my profile and start swiping on the first app. For the first hour or so, it's fun. I select the setting to show me people of all genders, and I have fun flipping through everyone's profiles. Then, I try another app, marveling at the similarities to and differences from the previous one.

By the time my friends retire into their bedroom, though, my fingers hurt. My vision is blurry. Head pounding, I flip through the people I've already matched with. Some have already sent me messages, but most of them are unfortunately very cringey. I openly mentioned I'm bi on my profile, which seemed like a good idea at the time. But I deeply regret it now, since a good chunk of the messages in my inbox are asking about threesomes.

I'm not necessarily opposed to threesomes, and maybe

if I were more adventurous or still in my early twenties, I'd actually have joined one. But there's something very icky about the fact that people just *assumed* I was into threesomes because I'm bisexual, like my sexuality is a porn category and not intrinsically part of my identity.

Somehow, being bi makes dating apps worse. Sure, I get to flip through hot people of multiple genders, but that doesn't necessarily mean I get more quality matches.

With a frustrated growl, I toss my phone to the opposite side of the couch. Is this really what modern technology has come to? All these innovations and we still haven't found a more effective way to meet people? No wonder we get so many questions about online dating on our advice column.

I'm about to call it a night when my phone buzzes. It's a notification from one of the apps. Most of the messages that aren't directly asking for a threesome are just "hey" or "how's it going?" but this one looks promising.

Hey, love your smile, it reads. Would like to take you out for drinks sometime if you're down? The guy's name is Craig, and I'm so tempted to crack a joke about Craigslist in my reply. But I don't, of course.

I scroll through his profile. He's a redhead, five feet ten, and works in tech, like many other guys do in the area. His pictures tell me that he likes football, has a good mix of guy and girl friends, and has a cute but generic Labrador retriever.

I shoot him a reply, Hey, Craig! How's your night going? I'd love to meet up sometime. When are you available this week?

His reply is almost instant. How about Saturday?

Sure! Here's my number.

A few seconds later, I get a text from an unknown number.

Hey, beautiful, it says.

Okay, I think. *A little direct, but not the worst first text I could have gotten.*

Hey! I type. After a moment of hesitation, I add on a smiley face before I press send.

And then, Craig sends me a picture of his dick.

When I open the message, it takes me a few seconds to even process what I'm seeing. I'm no stranger to dicks, but the sheer ridiculousness of my current pink-and-hairy situation renders me speechless. My day keeps getting more and more ridiculous.

I text my friends, I think I got my first dick pic.

The door to my friends' bedroom immediately slams open.

Kiara storms out first, wearing the satin scarf she wraps over her hair whenever she goes to bed. "Oh my *God.* Are you serious?"

"Yup," I reply. "I'd show you, but I know how you feel about dicks."

Kiara makes a gagging sound, like she's about to throw up. "Yeah, no, please don't."

Val follows Kiara, shaking her head. "See, this is why I don't date men anymore. But I can evaluate the dick if you want me to. For science."

We all laugh. Before Kiara and I met Val, she used to date men. Or, as she said once, "play video games with them and then end up fucking." She doesn't consider herself bi like me, though. Just a late bloomer lesbian that was previously yet another victim of comp het. Now, as a long-running joke, she likes to say, "This is why I don't date men anymore," whenever she sees a guy doing something stupid.

"I don't think I'm cut out for dating apps," I bemoan as my friends sit down next to me on Clementine.

Kiara looks down at her smartwatch. "Well, it's been less than six hours since you downloaded them! You're totally valid for wanting to quit after what happened with Craig, but maybe try going on at least one date? With someone else, of course. Not Craig."

"No shade if you do decide to go with Craig, though. If you liked what you saw," Val adds jokingly. "But also, as an IT professional, I must warn you that the dick pic he sent might not even be his. It could be a random image he found on Google. Or worse, an AI-generated one. Those are getting more and more realistic by the day."

Kiara shrieks, and we all laugh.

"Maybe I should try meeting people out in the wild, first," I say. "So far, dating apps don't seem like they're for me."

"That's a great idea," Kiara replies. "We're free tomorrow night, aren't we, babe? Since it'll be a Thursday. Why don't we all go out to a bar or something?"

"Sure, sounds good," Val says. "Gemma, do you know anywhere that's still doing those spiced fall cocktails? I've been getting my annual pumpkin spice latte craving but haven't gotten the chance to get one yet this year since I hardly ever go out."

Kiara and I snicker as we look at each other. Val likes

making fun of what she says are "basic bitch" things, but the one thing she can *never* resist is a good pumpkin spice latte. Or PSL-inspired cocktails. And of course, given what I do for a living, she asks me for recs on where to get one every year.

I smile. "I know just the place!"

Gemma

Fortunately, the next day at work isn't nearly as bad as the previous, mainly because I have something to look forward to at the end of it. Luckily, both James and Daphne seem dead set on *mostly* ignoring me, with the only moment of drama occurring when James wrinkles his nose after our eyes accidentally meet on my way to the elevator.

"At least I'm not the one making out with a coworker in the printer room!" I want to yell at him. But I obviously don't.

Shane also seems pretty content with whatever arrangement he must have worked out with James, because he just gives me a friendly "Hey, Gemma!" when we cross paths. Either that or he wants to pretend that nothing happened. Which is understandable.

I throw myself into my work again. Aside from the lifestyle recommendation articles, which are always fun, my favorite part of my job is reading the stories behind the people asking for advice on Dear Karl. I truly, deeply love all the different stories I read about other people's life experiences, and today, I find myself especially immersed in a submission from a man in his fifties who's trying to make the holidays good again for a woman whose husband died around this time last year. Thanksgiving is next week, so we've been getting a lot of advice requests about the holidays.

Love isn't dead, after all. Or at least, it isn't for some people.

I bookmark the man's email for now, along with some other messages I received about upcoming holiday events around the city. Providing a list of cute date ideas seems like the right approach, but I want to double-check with one of my Gen X coworkers first.

After work, Kiara, Val, and I bundle up in our coats and walk to the Financial District. It's only a fifteen-minute walk, but it seems much longer than that, especially since we have to walk past the condo I used to live in with James.

My friends know where I lived, but I don't want to make a big deal out of it. Not today. As an attempt to distract us all—and because I finally feel ready to talk about it—I launch into the story of what I saw in the printer room. Kiara's jaw drops, and Val fumes and cusses enough for all three of us, even throwing a few Spanish curse words here and there.

My friends' indignant reactions are thankfully enough

of a distraction that I only feel a slight twinge when the condo comes into view.

"Thank God you're not with him anymore," Kiara says finally. "This breakup was a blessing in disguise."

"Truly," Val agrees. "Thank you, next!"

They laugh, and I try my best to smile along with them. I must not be successful at hiding my pain, though, because Val pats me on the back as we join the line of young professionals that's already begun to form in front of our first destination, a bar called Rousseau's.

Rousseau's has been recommended by our "Places to Go for Seasonal Drinks" roundup in our lifestyle section for several years now. I'm not a big seasonal drinks person, so Shane usually covers them, but I'm still impressed by how there's already a line out the door at not even five thirty p.m. Their drinks must be *really* good.

When it's our turn to go in, Val holds the door open for Kiara and me.

As far as appearances go, Rousseau's is a standard, no-frills place, resembling more of a pub with its brick wall and dark wood bar top. When we were still together, James usually preferred to go to more bougie establishments with high ceilings and fancy backlit drink displays, so I'm relieved this isn't the kind of bar we'd see him in.

"Apparently their seasonal drinks are the best in the city, so I figured this would be a good place to start," I say as we follow the hostess to one of the high tables in the middle of the room.

"Yay!" Kiara exclaims. She claps her hands, and Val pumps her fists with excitement.

I order a plain espresso martini, while Kiara gets spiced apple fizz and Val orders her pumpkin spice cocktail. After we get our drinks, I look around. In this crowded, noisy space, it finally hits me. This is my first time at a bar as a single woman in *seven years*. I fidget in my seat, feeling a bit awkward. Hopefully it's not too obvious.

I look around. All the women around us are gathered in groups or pairs, like we are. And the last thing I want to do is barge in on a date or a friend gathering. I glance at the bar to see if there are any loners and spot a man who is an absolute giant. He has to be at least six foot five. As far as I can tell, he's sitting by himself at the bar as he sips on his old-fashioned. Since I'm five three and don't want to constantly look like a hobbit next to him, his height is automatically a deal-breaker for me for anything serious. But he's good-looking enough for me to consider something casual.

"Do you see someone you like?" Kiara asks, her voice hushed with excitement.

"Yup." I down my drink and immediately regret it when I feel the burn of the alcohol going down my throat. With a wince, I say, "Wish me luck."

"Godspeed," Val replies, making Kiara and me laugh.

Before I lose my resolve, I let out a quiet breath and head toward the giant.

"Hi," I say, extending a hand. "I'm Gemma. Pleasure to meet you."

The man raises his eyebrows, and it only then occurs to me that my greeting may have been too professional for a casual bar setting. I could not have made it any more obvious that this is my first night out as a single woman since *college*.

Fortunately, the man eventually says, "Hey." He takes my hand, which looks ridiculously tiny in his, and gently shakes it. "Ian. Nice to meet you."

For a split second, I'm afraid he's going to just go back to his drink, but Ian slowly scoots over to make room for me. He looks miserably cramped. This place wasn't designed for a person his size.

I sit down on the stool next to him.

"How are you?" I ask, jumping right into it. I hate small talk, but I hate awkward silences even more. "Do you work around here? How was your day?"

"Yeah," he replies with a shrug. "I work in finance, so, nothing too exciting. But my day's much better now that you're here with me."

He says the last part with a cheeky grin. After seven years of being in a relationship with the same person, a pickup line from a stranger is jarring. Laughable, even. But it isn't entirely unpleasant.

I give Ian my best coy smile. "Oh yeah? Well, I'm glad. Happy to be here."

His grin widens, and he gives me total bedroom eyes. Admittedly, it's really hot.

I could get used to this, I think.

Our night is almost too perfect. Ian and I make each other laugh. We talk about everything from cute dogs to world events. Best of all, he keeps the drinks flowing, consistently asking the bartender for refills whenever our glasses are almost empty.

Could it be this easy? I find myself thinking in my tipsy stupor. *Could I have struck gold on my first night out?* After my rough foray into dating apps the previous night, I want to weep with joy.

But then, of course, Ian drops the bomb.

"So," he says, slightly slurring his words. "I have to be honest with you. I feel like we do have a great connection but... I'm not looking for anything serious. I'd love to keep spending the night with you, though, if you're down for some fun?"

He nervously smiles while waiting for me to respond.

I swig back a cold glass of water and put it down on the bar top. Here I go. "That's fine," I say. "I just got out of a long-term relationship, so I'm looking for something casual, too. Want to head out?"

All the hesitation instantly disappears from Ian's face, making me wonder if it was all an act. With a smirk, he says, "Sure. We can take an Uber to my place."

Faint alarms sound in my head. I need to sober up.

"Great," I reply. "Let me freshen up a bit in the restroom before we go."

"Cool."

As soon as I'm out of Ian's line of sight, I lightly slap my cheeks on my way to the restroom. I might be feeling reckless, but that doesn't mean I want to be too incapacitated to call for help if Ian turns out to be a serial killer.

The bar is completely packed, so I'm surprised there isn't a line for the women's restroom. In fact, bizarrely enough, the hallway leading to the restroom is completely empty. And it doesn't take long for me to figure out why.

"You asshole!" a woman shouts, her words coming out slurred. "I should have known you—"

The distinct stench of vomit hits me like a thick, revolting wall when I open the bathroom door, along with the shrieks—and retches—of a woman in the innermost stall. I'm about to ask her if she needs help, when I hear another woman's voice.

"I'm sorry things turned out this way, Gretchen. I really am—"

My ears twitch. I've heard that voice before, but where?

"Fuck you!" Gretchen cuts in.

Oh God. If I weren't sober before, I definitely am now. It's just my luck to walk into an explosive breakup tonight out of all nights. At this rate, if a clown came unicycling down the hall, juggling little balls shaped like broken hearts, I wouldn't be surprised.

For some of us, romance *is* dead.

I'm tempted to leave and not butt into their business, but I decide to stay out of my concern for Gretchen. Girl code still exists, right? Even when the person who caused the mess is another woman.

I also want to know why the other woman sounds *so familiar.*

After splashing water onto my face at the bathroom sink

and drying myself off with a brown paper towel, I pinch my nose with two fingers and approach the last stall.

The door is unlocked, as if, in the chaos, both women forgot to lock it behind them. When I knock and push through, I realize where I've heard the other woman's voice. Many times before.

"Celeste?" I ask. "Is that you?"

Gemma

There's a Korean word, *inyeon*, for the fated destiny between two people. And apparently Celeste and I have that, but *agyeon*, or the bad kind that leaves you tossing and turning at night, because there's no other explanation I can think of for the stall door opening to reveal Celeste Min, my ex from college. She's holding back Gretchen's hair as she vomits, but both women straighten when they see me.

Gretchen wipes her mouth, flushes the toilet, and then fixes me with an icy, but slightly unfocused, glare. "Who are you?" she asks.

But before I can answer her, Celeste says, "Gem."

Her low, alto voice caresses every consonant of my name, sending chills down my spine.

Celeste was always beautiful, with large doe eyes made sharp by her signature winged eyeliner and long, elegant limbs. But the youthful awkwardness I remember her having back in college is gone, replaced by the goddess-like air of a fully defined woman almost in her thirties. Her entire body looks different now, toned and with the kind of ass you can only get from spending countless hours at the gym. Instead of the long waves that softened her features when we were younger, her hair is now pulled tight into a straight, sleek ponytail, accentuating her perfect jawline.

And her tattoos. Holy shit, Celeste has tattoos now.

Tattoos aren't widely accepted in Korean society, or at least not as much as they are in the US. When I was growing up, my parents would tell me only criminals and other social deviants have tattoos. That isn't to say no one in South Korea has tattoos—a good number do. But it's much more of a big "fuck you" to traditional values than it is here in the US, especially prominently visible ones like Celeste's. And definitely more so if you're a woman.

Gorgeously inked black flowers trail across her left arm and leg, giving her femme fatale vibes that make my heart skip a beat. I get the sudden urge to run my hands over them, to trace all the lines and curves.

But of course, I can't do that. Not when it's been eight years since we last saw each other.

I swallow, and ball my hands into fists before glancing away like I didn't spend the last few seconds staring at her. My cheeks are red-hot, but I keep my expression indifferent. That and avoiding eye contact are the only things I can do to keep some semblance of my pride.

But fuck. Some people *do* age like fine wine.

In an attempt to regain my sanity, I pretend Celeste doesn't exist, and address Gretchen instead.

"Sorry for barging in, but I wanted to check if you're okay," I say to her. "I can get you some water if you want..."

Gretchen heaves a long sigh and stumbles forward, away from Celeste. She jabs a finger in my direction and says, still slurring her words, "*You.* How do you know Celeste? She's been cheating on me this whole time, hasn't she?"

And that's enough drama for me today. It appears I overstepped. Gretchen has stopped vomiting, at least, so it's time for me to make my exit.

I back away, pushing the stall door open behind me. "Um, no idea about the second part but if she was, it wasn't with me. We went to college together, that's all. I haven't seen her in eight years."

I of course don't mention she's my ex. That's a detail I doubt will sit well with Gretchen.

If Celeste visibly reacts to what I say, I don't see it, because I force myself to keep ignoring her. Her mere presence, only a few feet away, makes my entire body tingle in an unfortunately not-unpleasant way. I can't stay here.

Some part of me wants to yell at Celeste like Gretchen's been doing and demand that she explain why she left me all those years ago. Why everyone in my life keeps *leaving* me without any explanation whatsoever. But I know she's not the type to respond well to that kind of thing. Admittedly, few people are, but Celeste is even more allergic to loud voices and conflict than anyone I've ever known. Or at least, she was eight years ago.

Celeste shifts her weight, and I instinctively glance in her direction. *Damn it.*

Apparently, she's been watching me this entire time. But when our eyes meet, hers immediately dart back to Gretchen.

"I didn't cheat," she says, quietly but firmly. "Please don't think that. Just because I don't do relationships—which I made clear when we first met—doesn't mean I'm a cheater."

I make a sound of disbelief before I can stop myself. Both Gretchen and Celeste give me confused looks, but I couldn't help it. The Celeste I knew was a hopeless romantic. She was the girl who carried around romance books and made little braids in my hair when we were curled up in bed together. The girl who whispered how much she loved me and wanted to marry me one day. And now, she doesn't "do relationships"? What *happened*?

"Can you please leave?" asks Gretchen, shooting me a glare. "We're in the middle of something here."

She doesn't need to tell me twice. Successfully avoiding eye contact with Celeste this time around, I slip out of the restroom. This is clearly not the time and place for me to interrogate Celeste about her past. About *our* past. Especially not after the night I've had.

And that's when I remember what I was doing before Celeste crashed into my life again.

Oh shit. I glance down at my phone.

I'd received a couple texts from Kiara and Val asking me if I'm okay. I immediately reply to them to say that I am, and Kiara tells me they're now at another bar down the street.

You're welcome to join us if you want! she writes.

I'll see you guys back at the apartment, I reply. Thanks for coming out with me!

Of course! Kiara replies.

Have fun~ texts Val. While also being safe, of course.

We'll stay in this area for the next hour or so before heading back home, so just call or text us if anything happens! Kiara adds.

I tap my phone to heart Kiara's message and make my way through the bar, doing a double take when I see Ian angrily yelling at the bartender for more drinks. He seemed tipsy when I left, but now he's *definitely* drunk.

The rage disappears from his face the moment he sees me.

"Oh, you didn't leave?" he asks sheepishly.

"Nope," I say. "Sorry, I was helping someone in the bathroom."

"Oh." He puts down his empty glass.

"Sorry. I should have let you know." I turn to the bartender, a blue-haired twenty-something with piercings, and add, "*So* sorry you had to deal with this."

I fish a couple of bills from my wallet and place them on the bar. The bartender gratefully slips the money into their pocket.

Ian is practically a stranger, but I still don't want to leave him alone at the bar like this. Not when he's drunk out of his mind. Maybe I can call him a car.

"Come on," I say to Ian. "Let's get you out of here."

I meant those last words figuratively, since there's no way I can actually physically take him out of the bar, and am wholly unprepared when Ian slumps forward, slipping down from his seat like he expects someone like me to support a giant like him.

"Oh, nononono!"

Panic flashes in my head, but I'm not fast enough to avoid the crushing weight of a two-hundred-something-pound man bearing down on me. It's like I'm fighting a grizzly. And failing miserably.

The people around us jump out of the way. A few younger ones start recording on their phones. This is what I get for trying to be nice. Which is laughable now, because clearly, no one wants to help *me*.

I'm about to drop him on the floor when the pressure lightens significantly.

"Whoa there, buddy."

I turn my head to see Celeste holding the man up. Her slender arms strain against his weight, but they miraculously push a now asleep Ian back onto the bar stool. The jackass actually dozed off at some point.

Still, Celeste manhandled him expertly...all while wearing *heels*. It's, unfortunately, one of the hottest things I've ever seen in my life.

My face heats up when our eyes met again. *Shit.*

"I never understood why short women always go for the really tall guys," Celeste says in a familiar, dry tone. "Save some for us tall girls, won't you, Gemma?"

I'm out of breath, and my heart is still racing with the adrenaline of having almost been crushed alive. But I manage to get out, "You don't even like men."

Celeste flashes me a wry smile. "That's incorrect. I like

my jiujitsu instructor *and* my personal trainer, and without both *men*, we would have been crushed alive. Not all of them are bad, shockingly. My best friend is also a guy."

Shoving away all inappropriate thoughts of Celeste working out and wrestling with people on the floor, I clear my throat. "But you'd never date them."

She cocks her head to the side in acknowledgment.

"Where's Gretchen?" I ask, belatedly realizing that the other woman is nowhere to be found.

"Safely on her way home. I got her a car."

Celeste's words echo in my head. *I don't do relationships.*

"So," I start to ask. "What happened—"

"Are you two together?" Celeste cuts in before I can finish my question. It takes me a moment to realize she's talking about Ian.

"No, I just met the guy. This is kind of our first date."

I glance down at the now unconscious man. From this angle, he looks unexpectedly cute, almost like a big, sleeping baby and not the massive giant he really is.

"Wow, some first date," Celeste replies.

Now that Ian's out of the way, I can't ignore how close she and I are to each other. It's still hard to believe she's standing *right here* in this random bar in San Francisco. I could lean over and kiss her if I wanted to.

Before I can stop myself, my eyes linger on her scarlet-red-painted lips.

"How about you?" I ask. "Why are you here? I thought you moved back to Seoul."

Celeste leans back against the bar. "I did. But I came

back to LA a year later to finish my degree. Now, I travel back and forth between there and SF for my photography work. I got in yesterday for another project here."

The bartender turns back to us, and Celeste orders a pumpkin spice cocktail, the same drink Val ordered when my friends and I arrived at the bar.

"And what happened between you and Gretchen?" I can't resist asking.

A crease appears between Celeste's eyebrows. "Pretty much what you heard in the restroom" is the only thing she says in response. The bartender hands Celeste her drink, and she takes a long sip.

I expect her to go on, to tell me about why she doesn't do relationships or why she disappeared on me so many years ago, but she doesn't. She slowly takes another sip of her cocktail instead, keeping her gaze on the floor. I'm about to directly ask her about everything she clearly doesn't want to talk about when something she'd said earlier gives me pause.

"Wait, what project?"

She shrugs. "Oh, it's for some magazine. They want me to shoot video and take photos of couples for Valentine's Day. It doesn't start until later, but I had to meet with some people to finalize some things. I *could* have done the meeting virtually but since I had another shoot in the area scheduled for this weekend, I figured I'd come in earlier and kill two birds with one stone."

And then it all clicks. The Valentine's Day project that I've been assigned to. The hot woman photographer from

UCLA that Kiara mentioned. And now, Celeste, who's not in Seoul or Los Angeles but in San Francisco, of all places, sitting right next to me in this crowded bar.

"No," I whisper. It's all I can do against the wave of horror that rushes over me.

Celeste cocks her head in confusion, her eyes squinting with concern. "You okay?"

A whirlwind of thoughts and emotions war inside me. I want to scream. To laugh. To do both at the same time. But what I *don't* want to do is tell Celeste that we're assigned to work together. That's an awkward conversation I won't be touching with a ten-foot pole.

I have to get out of here and email Evelyn. I resolve to meet with her as soon as I can and change her mind about hiring Celeste. I might not be able to do anything about the past, but I want to do everything in my power to stop our paths from messily overlapping again.

"Well, thanks for your help," I say. "Have a good rest of your night. I'm taking this guy home."

I'm not, but the lie is a hundred percent worth Celeste's reaction. She jerks back in disgust, a way stronger reaction than I expected from her.

"Wait, you're going home with this loser?" she asks.

"That's the plan, or at least, it was before I got caught up in all of this," I say, gesturing between her and me.

"Do you even know where he lives?"

I shrug. "I'll ask him."

When I shake him awake, he gives me an address on Spear Street, a less-than-ten-minute drive from the bar.

I turn to Celeste with a triumphant smile. "Well, there you go."

I'm trying to flag down the bartender when I feel a firm but gentle grip on my shoulder.

"Gem," Celeste says, her voice low and smooth like silk. "This is crazy. You barely know this guy *and* he's half-asleep. You should get him a taxi or something and go home."

I check the time on my phone to avoid telling Celeste that I'm actually doing exactly what she said I should do. *Ten fifty-five p.m.* After disappearing without any explanation or apology for *eight years*, who does she think she is to tell me what I can or can't do?

I type Ian's address into my phone and request a ride. Luckily the cost is pretty minimal since it's not rush hour.

"Can I have two glasses of water, please?" I ask when the bartender turns our way. "And close the tab? Sorry, again."

"It happens," they congenially say as they pour two glasses of water for us and place the check on the bar.

I chug the first glass of water and press the other one against Ian's cheek to wake him up. I *really* don't want to pay for his egregious bill.

Fortunately, Ian stirs awake.

"Oh, hello!" he says. "Sorry, did I pass out?"

"Yup, but don't worry about it. Let's go. Don't forget to pay your bill!"

I keep my tone light and friendly, and Ian dutifully pays without incident—*thank God.* As we get up to leave, he catches sight of Celeste, who's been closely watching him this entire time like a murderous cat.

"Wait, who's she?"

I almost call Celeste a "friend" but then realize she's everything but. And I don't want to get into our painful history with a total stranger, either, so I say, "Just someone I know."

As Ian and I leave, I fix Celeste with one last stare. She blinks rapidly, her eyes widening slightly as she bites her bottom lip. It's an innocent gesture, but the sudden moment of vulnerability makes my cheeks heat up again. I quickly turn away and walk out the bar with Ian.

When his car arrives, I hold the door open.

"You're not coming with me?" Ian asks, pouting like a little kid.

"Sorry," I say. "Maybe some other night."

I have no intention of ever seeing this guy again, but I don't want to piss him off. You can never tell how men will react to rejection, and I've already seen him yell at someone once tonight.

Luckily, Ian is either too tired or too drunk to put up much of a fight. He obediently slips into the back seat, and I close the door behind him.

The car drives off, leaving me alone with thoughts of Celeste.

Once upon a time in college, Celeste Min fell in love with a girl named Gemma.

Gemma Cho was a friend of a friend, and they'd only ended up rooming together because Kayla Peterson, Celeste's roommate of two years, spontaneously moved in with her boyfriend the summer before junior year. Since she felt bad for ditching her, Kayla brought in her other friend, Gemma, to replace her in the apartment they'd already signed the lease for.

Celeste hadn't minded, especially after she saw how pretty Gemma was. Since Kayla, a Taylor Swift look-alike who now has three kids with her own Travis Kelce, was—and still is—one of Celeste's straightest friends, Celeste had assumed Gemma only liked guys, too. But then she realized that, while she couldn't stop staring at the beautiful girl she'd somehow ended up living with, the girl was also staring back at *her*.

Gemma told Celeste that she'd never dated a girl before. But after countless days and nights of going on dreamlike dates around LA and whispering sweet nothings in each other's ears, Celeste had hoped she was the exception.

Now, alone in a dark, crowded bar in San Francisco, she sips her drink.

Celeste had never expected to see Gemma again, not after Celeste's mom got sick and she had to temporarily drop out of school.

For her first four months back home, Celeste drowned, floundering in medical trauma and familial expectations. She only survived because of Min-joon, her best friend in Seoul, who, as a bi man also from a deeply traditional family, could understand her struggles of taking care of someone who never fully accepted who she is.

But nothing could mitigate the intense pain and betrayal Celeste felt when she'd finally managed to pull herself back to the surface, only to discover that Gemma had not only moved on, but she'd moved on with a man. A lesbian's worst nightmare.

Since then, Celeste had refused to do relationships, a rule that Gretchen Sanders had blatantly ignored. But Celeste can't exactly blame Gretchen. It's only natural for someone to think they would be the exception, that they would be the one to change someone else and achieve that pipe dream happily ever after.

After all, Celeste once thought she was special, too.

6

Gemma

"Absolutely not." Evelyn's response comes quick and without a moment of hesitation. "All the paperwork just got finalized, and we're already behind schedule. Plus, she's perfect for the project, so I'm not sure why choosing someone else is even necessary. I had a lunch meeting with her yesterday, and she was absolutely lovely."

I tightly clutch my thermos of coffee, trying to find the right words to explain the situation to Evelyn.

"What if I have a... personal reason why I can't work with her?" I ask, keeping my voice as steady as I can. "She and I have history, and not a good one at that."

Peering at me over the edge of her glasses in a way that reminds me of Meryl Streep in *The Devil Wears Prada*, Evelyn purses her lips. "What kind of history?" she asks, slowly drawing out every word.

I sigh. So much for keeping my personal life away from my professional one.

"We dated," I say. "In college. Things didn't end well, and honestly, if I knew she was attached to this project, I would have asked to not be assigned to it."

I drink from my thermos as Evelyn raises her eyebrows. "That bad? So you still have feelings for her."

I splutter, choking on a mouthful of coffee.

"Um, no, of course I don't. It's been almost ten years since we dated. I've been engaged to and broken up with a whole other person since the last time we saw each other."

"Well, I'm assuming working with Ms. Min won't be a problem, then?" Evelyn asks, turning her attention back to her desktop. If it weren't for the slight, amused quirk of her lips, I'd think she's being dismissive.

She thinks it's funny, I realize. And I guess, in a hilariously cruel twist of fate kind of way, it is. I think back to how awkward things were between Celeste and me last night.

"Gemma, if it bothers you that much, I can certainly assign this project to another writer," Evelyn goes on when I don't say anything else. "Since Celeste is already contracted to be on this project, the only movement we can do at this point is internal. But I'd much prefer the writer to be *you*, since it's an amazing opportunity."

Disappointment flashes in her eyes. Evelyn's done so much for me in the last seven years. She's probably the reason why I still have this job in the first place. I hate letting her down, so I blurt out, "It's not just me, though. I mean, I can handle it, if I have to. But if Celeste knew I'm involved in the project, she wouldn't want to stay on it, either."

It's hardly a lie. Celeste *had* seemed as uncomfortable around me last night as I was with her. Maybe even more.

"Oh?" Evelyn asks. "If that's the case, it can't be helped. Could you please reach out to her and ask her to confirm? Sorry, Gemma. I have a meeting in five. You can cc me on the email if you'd like. I'll step in if needed."

As if on cue, Evelyn's phone rings. She picks up and says, "Yes?"

With her other hand, she jots down an email address onto the back of her own business card before handing it to me as she continues talking to the person on the other line. "Understood. I'm on my way. Thank you."

I blush, realizing how ridiculous and unprofessional I must seem right now, making a big deal about a work assignment because of a college ex. Fortunately, Evelyn seems to find it amusing, and she and I have a long enough working relationship that this isn't something she'd fire me over. Or at least, I hope not.

Mouthing *Thank you* to Evelyn, I slip out of her office, carrying the business card with my arm stretched out in front of me like I'm handling a vicious viper. Honestly, I would have rather it be an actual snake than a piece of paper with Celeste's email address. At least then I'd know what kind of situation I'm getting myself into.

Despite the awkwardness, Celeste seemed polite enough when I saw her yesterday, so hopefully the email exchange will be quick and painless. Hands trembling, I open Outlook and write up the most professional email I can manage.

From: gemmacho@citrine.com
To: celestemin@celestemin.com
CC: evelnynsanderson@citrine.com
Subject: Modern Love in Focus

Hi, Celeste. This is Gemma. I heard we're bringing you into this project. Unfortunately, I'm also attached to it. It's understandable if you don't want to work with me. Let us know and we'll make changes.

Best,
Gem

I'm about to hit send when, last minute, I add the last "ma" to the end of my name. "Gem" is what Celeste called me when we were dating. It's also what she called me last night.

Old habits only die when you kill them with force.

During lunch, I get a text from Mom. Since she prefers phone calls, she and I don't usually text, and especially not during work hours. But when I read the notification, I realize I haven't talked to my parents since I first told them about my breakup with James.

I can sense all her concerns, fears, and love in the three words she sends.

Have you eaten?

We're so Korean sometimes, it hurts. In our culture, food is absolutely a love language, and it's deeply ingrained in our history and how people often went hungry as war tore the land apart. My parents rarely ask me how I'm feeling, but they always ask me if I've eaten my meals.

All things considered, I'm glad. "Have you eaten?" is a much easier question to answer than "Are you okay?" I wouldn't have the slightest clue how to respond to the latter.

I'm about to, I reply. And then in a second message I add, Thanks. I'll come home for Thanksgiving.

She sends me back a big, red heart, and I do a quick search of flights from SFO to SNA. Since it's a smaller airport, flights to John Wayne are often pricey and limited, especially during the holidays. But I definitely do not want to ask my sixty-something parents to drive for over an hour in heavy traffic to pick me up from LAX.

The last time I visited my parents was in September for Chuseok, the Korean Mid-Autumn Festival. James and I flew down together. Even then, I had no idea I'd be coming home again so soon, on Thanksgiving, since for the last seven years, James and I always drove down to San Jose to celebrate the holiday with *his* family.

While my parents do a simple but still delicious meal whenever we celebrate the holidays together, the

Mathesons always threw extravagant parties in their mansion with tons of relatives and acquaintances. Aside from a few of the servers and other staff, I'd often be the only non-white person there, which initially made me uncomfortable. But after the first couple of years, I got used to it, and thankfully, even though we were clearly in very different tax brackets, everyone was usually super nice and sweet.

Daphne, who is not only white but also—if the office gossip is true—very rich, will probably fit right in from the start. My stomach turns at the thought.

I'm about to shut down my computer and leave the office for the day when I get Celeste's reply.

From: celeste@celestemin.com
To: gemmacho@citrine.com
CC: evelynsanderson@citrine.com
Subject: RE: Modern in Love in Focus Project

Hey, Gem. Nice to hear from you. I'm fine with being on the project if you are. Talk to you soon.

-C

Fuck. I read the email over and over again, as if my life depends on the few sentences. No, I'm *not* fine with any of this. But it's not like I have a choice. Not really. Evelyn is dead set on keeping Celeste. Like I said I would, I'll just have to deal with my own discomfort.

It'll be the biggest project you've ever worked on at Horizon, I remind myself.

I take a deep breath. The only thing I can do at this point is rip off the Band-Aid. I hit reply and write up another email.

From: gemmacho@citrine.com
To: celeste@celestemin.com
CC: evelynsanderson@citrine.com
Subject: RE: Modern Love in Focus

Hi, Celeste. Great! Then why don't we meet up sometime after Thanksgiving to talk more about our visions for the project, expectations, etc.? Let me know your availability.

-Gemma

In almost no time at all, Celeste sends me a list of her available days and times. Unfortunately, things are going as smooth as they can.

I glance up from the email chain and realize it's half past five. No way am I working overtime to schedule things with Celeste. On a Friday, no less. She'll have to wait until Monday morning.

I shut down my computer and head out for the weekend.

The days before Thanksgiving fly by in a blur, like they usually do, with everyone in the office either slacking off or working in hyperdrive before the holiday. I'm in the latter camp, and I hustle to get as much done as I can, including finalizing my meeting time with Celeste. Since she isn't coming back from LA until a full week after the holiday, the earliest time we can meet is the next Friday night. Which isn't ideal, but it can't be helped. We'll have to start working on the project ASAP after we meet.

On Thanksgiving morning, I fly an hour and a half to Irvine. The gravity of the whole situation only fully sinks in when I see my parents' worried faces at the airport. In the seven years I've lived in SF, it was always either Mom or Dad who came to pick me up, never both. The fact that they're both here, even after I called ahead to tell them I'd get an Uber back home, is a crushing reminder of how much my life has changed since I last saw them.

Mom envelops me in her arms. Dad follows suit, and even without them saying anything, I can tell they can feel my grief as if it were their own.

Neither of my parents say "We told you so" on the drive back home. Nor do they say something like "See, this is why we told you to date a nice Korean man from our church." They don't say anything, other than to ask how Val and Kiara are doing and if I'd eaten dinner yet.

I must look more pathetic than I thought.

Back home, Mom's prepared us an extravagant meal of braised beef galbi, pan-fried dumplings, japchae noodles, and more than five different other side dishes that make my mouth water. We've never been the traditional American Thanksgiving type of family, opting to eat Korean food for every holiday instead.

When we don't have any guests over and it's just the three of us, Mom usually only makes one nice dish, like a hearty stew or banquet noodles. Without her even having to tell me, I know she's put in extra effort today to help me feel better.

My heart squeezes in the best way.

"Eat up," Mom says. "You've lost a lot of weight since we saw you last."

Korean mom translation: *You don't look well. I'm worried about you.*

Over dinner, my parents and I catch up, talking in a mix of both Korean and English like we always do. They tell me what they've been up to, both at work and in their Korean church community, and I tell them as much as I can about what happened in my life—minus printer room–gate and my messy bar encounters—without bursting into tears. They're worried enough about me as it is. I don't want them to lose sleep at night because of my dating woes.

Hours later, after they've gone to bed, I draw myself a bath. When I was a kid, Mom used to draw one for me whenever I'd had a particularly hard day at school. I'd come home feeling like the world was imploding and submerge myself into hot water infused with whatever bath salts Mom was into that day. By the time I got out of the tub, life would feel manageable again, like I'd finished a therapy session.

I haven't taken a bath since the breakup, because I didn't want to rack up my friends' water bills. So when I sink into the soothingly warm water tonight, I relish it. Or at least, I try to. But no matter how much I stay submerged or scrub away my dead skin, I can't change the fact that I gave up seven years of my life for someone who seemingly had a change of heart overnight. I can't change the fact that just weeks after my disastrous and traumatic breakup, I ran into my college ex. And I can't change the fact that she and I will have to see each other regularly until we finish working on "Modern Love in Focus."

If Celeste and I weren't already exes, it'd be like a meet-cute of a rom-com. But instead, it's more like a car crash. An accidental encounter between two people who would rather not have been at the same place at the same time.

When the water grows cold, I get up from the tub, dry off, and change into pajamas. Then I slip into my childhood bed with my phone in one hand. Like I've been doing for the past few weeks, I search for and apply to "roommate wanted" listings in the city. There's no way I can afford to live by myself in San Francisco, so this is the best I can do for now.

After I run out of listings to apply for, I end up flipping through people's Instagram Stories and feel a slight sting of FOMO when I see Kiara, Val, and their other friends at a queer Friendsgiving party. They all look so happy, an emotion that seems foreign to me right now.

I exit out of my friends' stories to go to my own profile. Tragically, my last post was a picture of James and me laughing together while wine tasting in Napa with his parents in October. James's *mom* took this picture. And both our faces—mine a little flushed from the alcohol—are so bright and cheery.

My big, gaudy engagement ring shines bright in the sunlight.

I pinch my phone screen with both hands to zoom into the picture, scrutinizing James's smile. It looks so *genuine*, which ironically makes me feel better about my situation. At least it isn't obvious that James wanted to end our relationship. Or that he had any thoughts of doing so at all. Is it my fault that my ex either has the skills of an Emmy Award–winning actor or had a drastically sudden change of heart? My head hurts thinking about how, two weeks after this photo was taken, James would become just another ex.

I tap on the three dots in the top right corner and delete the photo.

Before I fully realize what I'm doing, I unblock Celeste on social media and navigate to her profile.

For the sake of my own mental well-being, I'd blocked her back when we first broke up. It's almost comical how easy it is to unblock her now, after eight years of keeping her tightly locked away in my past.

We're not following each other now, of course, but her account is public, so I can still see everything. I'm surprised to see that she has over five hundred *thousand* followers. When we dated, she didn't even have five hundred. I scroll through countless beautifully shot portraits, breathtaking pictures of Californian landscapes, and various promotional shoots with stunningly gorgeous models. I spot Gretchen in one of the shots, her long auburn hair glowing as she looks out at the Big Sur coastline during sunset.

So that's how they met.

I keep scrolling until Celeste's posts begin to blur together. Some naive part of me hopes that if I go far enough, I'll find the reason why Celeste left me so many years ago.

But of course, I don't.

Instead, toward the end of her page, I spot a picture that's practically a jump-scare. A selfie of Celeste and me, back in college, her lips gently pressed against my forehead as we lie together on a picnic blanket. Celeste is taking the photo, and I still remember the words she said as she snapped it: "Just commemorating how much I love my beautiful girlfriend."

We both look like *babies*, or at least, that's how we appear to present-day, twenty-nine-year-old me. Our cheeks are flushed and still round with baby fat, and neither Celeste nor I has a single visible wrinkle on our faces. I'd turned twenty-one a few months before this photo, and I remember thinking I was a real adult, now that I could legally drink. Which is entirely laughable to me now.

I thought I had everything figured out then, since by that point, Celeste and I were talking about "grown-up things" like a getting a place together in Koreatown after graduation. Just like twenty-nine-year-old me had no idea James Matheson would suddenly break off our engagement, twenty-one-year-old me had no idea Celeste would upend our lives and disappear.

By the time I close Instagram for the night, I've made my decision.

I can't work with Celeste until I know why she disappeared on me eight years ago. And I know just the place we can meet to talk about everything.

Gemma

The next Friday at around eight p.m., I enter through the doors of the Irishman's Jig, an Irish pub in San Francisco that my friends and I usually go to for St. Patrick's Day. Because I don't regularly frequent Irish pubs, I have no idea what they even do on normal weekdays, but it's the least romantic spot I could think of for Celeste and me to meet. And it's a fun enough place that I can't imagine myself crying in here if things go wrong. Or at least, I hope I won't.

Since it's the first week of December, the Irishman's Jig is decked out with Christmas lights, bright tinsel, and nutcracker statues. A handful of college students in red Santa suits and green elf costumes tune their fiddles and flutes on the stage. I watch them for a moment before looking around for Celeste.

When we were in college, Celeste was always perpetually

early for everything, so I'm not surprised to see her already sitting in the back corner of the pub like she's a regular. Maybe she is. Just thinking about how we've been in the same state for all these years, possibly frequenting the same places but at different times, makes my heart race. That's one piece of knowledge I wish I never found out about.

Today, Celeste looks gorgeous, even though she's just wearing a black leather jacket over a simple white shirt and jeans. I breathe a sigh of relief. I don't think I can survive another encounter with those ridiculously sexy tattoos of hers. I barely resisted the urge to run my fingers across her skin the last time I saw her.

When she sees me, Celeste holds up a hand in the air. I can't even meet her gaze without blushing. Which is an absolutely fan-fucking-tastic start. Eight years later and she still has that effect on me. I'm almost thirty and yet, around her, I'm a shy college kid again, my cheeks turning red whenever I accidentally make eye contact with my beautiful roommate.

"The Irishman's Jig, huh?" Celeste asks when I sit down across the table from her.

"A proud and historic establishment of the city, first opened in 1972." I point at the sign above the door that says just that.

"Ah, yes. The seventies. How historic," she says dryly, before nodding her head at the musicians behind me. "They're going to have a live performance soon. Are you okay with that?"

I purse my lips. The truth is, I hadn't even considered

the possibility of there being a performance on a normal weekday night. But it *is* a Friday, so maybe I should have known better. I shrug as nonchalantly as I can. "Sure, why not? We can take breaks from talking to watch, I guess. And go somewhere else if it gets too bad."

Celeste frowns. "Okay, then."

I clear my throat. "Before we work together, I need to go over some things with you."

Her eyebrows shoot up. "All right. What things?"

"First of all, I want you to know, I did everything I could to make it so we wouldn't have to work together. But unfortunately, Evelyn is convinced you're the perfect person for the job. And at this point, it's also too late to get someone else."

Celeste smirks, resting her chin on her right hand. "I knew I liked her."

Frustration rises up inside me like a kettle about to boil over.

"I need this project to do well, Celeste," I say, my voice coming out sharper than I intended. "If this doesn't get the attention we need, my coworkers and I might lose our jobs."

She sits up, finally serious. "This project is a big deal for me, too, so don't worry about that. Or at least, not about the visual aspect of it. And I'm willing to work with you, if you're willing to work with me."

Celeste takes out a tablet from her big black purse and opens it to a gallery of what I can only assume is her most recent work. I try to keep a blank face as I look at her portraits, practically holding my breath because I *cannot* let her know that I stalked her online and have already seen some of these pictures. Thankfully, a good chunk are portraits and videos that weren't shared on social media, featuring various individuals from all walks of life. All framed and lit perfectly, the people in her art somehow look both familiar and ethereal at the same time, like neighbors portrayed in a way that makes them appear otherworldly.

Like the pictures on her Instagram, all the pieces in her portfolio are beautiful, too. And I can now see why Evelyn thinks she's perfect for this job. My voice comes out hushed when I say, "You're really talented."

Our eyes meet over the small candle in the center of the table. Somehow, even amid all the people laughing and sloshing beer around us, it feels like Celeste and I are in the middle of our own romantic date.

Fortunately, at that exact moment, loud cheers erupt from the people seated around us. Everyone raises their pints of beer, and Celeste, with a bemused look on her face, raises her hand like she's holding an invisible drink.

Four dancers appear onstage, dressed in matching green shirts and either black skirts or leotard pants.

"Oh, this is going to be good," Celeste says. She stands up from her seat and whoops, joining in with the loud cheers. "Definitely not something you'd ever see in Korea. Well, maybe in Itaewon, but not anywhere else."

A server comes by our table, asking, "Do you two want to order any drinks before they start the performance?"

Celeste glances over at me. "You okay with drinking during our meeting? We don't have to if you don't want to."

I mull it over. I do want to keep things *relatively* professional. But it *is* a Friday night, and I'm going to need a drink by the time Celeste and I are done talking about everything. "Sure, why not?"

"Fabulous." Celeste turns her attention back to the server. "I'll have a Guinness, and she'll have a Blue Moon." She turns back to me. "You still like those, right?"

"Yeah," I say begrudgingly, before it hits me. "Wait, who said I was okay with you buying me a drink?"

She winks at me. "It's the least I can do for crashing your work project."

Celeste ordering me a drink *and* winking at me takes us dangerously close to the "date" category. When the server comes back with our beers, I take a small sip of mine. *Celeste* can get drunk and sloppy, for all I care. I'll gladly be the one to keep things professional.

The music starts, rendering all conversation impossible as everyone claps and stomps along to the dancers, who prance around the stage to the bright and cheery music. Some sound like traditional Irish songs, while others are classical renditions of holiday tunes.

The performance goes on for much longer than I expected it to, and even though it was my idea to come here in the first place, I start to regret it. I want to keep Celeste at arm's length, but we still have a lot of things we need to talk about. Namely, our past. Which won't be an easy conversation in the slightest.

I'm about to suggest to Celeste that we go somewhere else when I notice she's not at our table anymore. Somehow, she's linked arms with the guys at the table next to us. I watch as they dance in a circle and joyfully slosh their beer around.

Celeste's cheeks are bright pink, and my eyes almost instinctively drop down to her red-painted lips. When our gazes meet again, the corner of her mouth lifts. That small movement is enough to make me swallow.

The moment thankfully passes, and she turns around to laugh at something one of the guys said. The music is too loud for me to make out any words, but she replies, and suddenly the whole group is cracking up like she said the funniest joke in the world. One guy even slaps his knees and almost falls backward, which makes everyone laugh harder.

Somehow, she's already all buddy-buddy with these strangers, something I could never do. And that's when it hits me. Besides her technical skills, there's another reason why Celeste is absolutely perfect for this project.

I love my job because I can help strangers in heavily controlled environments, like answering virtual submissions and emails. But just because I love people doesn't mean I'm good with them. Meanwhile, even back in college, when she first started out by taking graduation photos to build her portfolio, Celeste somehow always knew the right words to say to make her clients drop their guards and loosen up. By the time she was done taking their photos, she not only became friends with all of them, but she captured her subjects in the best figurative *and* literal light, helping them shine in their own unique ways.

From the way she's instantly charmed her way into the group of guys, it's clear that Celeste still has those social skills. Meanwhile, since graduating from college, I haven't made any new friends other than Val and Kiara, whom I met several years ago.

The music finally comes to a stop, and the dancers bow as the audience gives them a round of applause.

"Thank you, everyone!" says one of the performers onstage. "We're done for the night but stick around for other great performances tonight. The Irish Fighters are up next, and they'll be ready in a few minutes. Happy Friday and happy holidays!"

After a round of resounding cheers, the college students get off the stage and everyone settles back into their seats. I'm watching the Irish Fighters, a local band whose lead singer looks suspiciously like Dave Grohl, set up their guitars and drums when Celeste says, "Whew. Sorry about that. This is my first time at an Irish pub, so I couldn't resist having some fun."

She gives me an impish smile, reminding me of why I first fell in love with her so many years ago. Sure, she's super sexy, but I was always even more attracted to her personality, the fun, air sign energy that kept her—and me, too, when I was dating her—leaping from new experience to new experience with a childlike sense of wonder.

That's something I'll always be grateful to Celeste for, no matter what. Realizing I'm not straight during junior year in college would have been a lot scarier if Celeste hadn't been there by my side, making everything, even my own sexuality, feel like just another fun adventure we were going on together.

In the now relatively quiet din of the Irish pub, I finally say, "Celeste. We have to talk about our past before we start this project. You may be able to pretend that nothing happened between us, but I can't see you all the time and *work with you* after what you did."

The smile drops from Celeste's face. She clears her throat and takes a swig of her beer.

There's a sharp edge in her voice when she asks, "What *I* did? Okay, sure. Let's talk about everything."

I tense up, preemptively preparing myself for her response. "Why did you disappear eight years ago?"

Celeste blinks, as if that's not what she expected me to say. Finally, with her gaze cast down to the floor, she says, "My mom got sick, so I had to go back home. Things were bad, so I couldn't return to the US to finish my degree until the next school year, after her condition stabilized a bit."

The way she explains it, it's so straightforward. But there's something off about her voice and the way she's avoiding my gaze as she speaks.

I frown. "Is your mom okay now?" I ask, fearing the worst.

Celeste's eyes widen. "Oh, yeah. She is. Or as well as she can be. She's in remission. Has been for several years now, thankfully."

"That's good to hear." I breathe a sigh of relief and sit back in my seat.

"What?" she asks when I don't say anything else.

"It's just..." It's my turn to look away, but instead of the floor, I stare at the stage where the Irish Fighters are setting up. "I wish you'd have come to me and told me what was going on with your mom, rather than break up with me via text with no explanation. It made me feel like I meant nothing to you. Also, it's been eight years. Like, I get that you had a lot going on when you first went back home, but what about afterward? You never replied to my messages on KakaoTalk asking if you were okay. And you dodged all my calls. You *ghosted* me, after we were together for over a year."

KakaoTalk is the chatting app that almost all Koreans use, whether they live in South Korea or elsewhere in the world. Even though I blocked her on social media, I kept that channel open between us for all these years and occasionally sent her messages, in case she ever decided to reach out. But she always read everything I sent her without replying.

Celeste stares down at her hands. "First of all, I'm sorry for leaving like that. Definitely not the best way to go about things. I fully acknowledge that. I was—still am—the only member of my family living abroad. And since that was the first time I experienced a family emergency, I panicked when I heard that my mom was in the hospital. I dumped my stuff at Goodwill on my way to the airport and didn't even properly withdraw from classes until I arrived in Seoul."

"Wow," I reply. "That's a lot."

She nods in acknowledgment before looking up from her drink. The sudden heat in her eyes is so intense that I'm taken aback as she says, "And as for why I didn't reach out later... honestly, I didn't even know you cared that much. You blocked me on social media and were already dating someone else *four months* after I left."

Gemma

For a second, I'm shocked to hear that Celeste knows about James. In my head, the two of them exist in separate universes. But we all went to the same school and had some of the same friends. Of course Celeste heard about him.

"Did Kayla tell you?" I ask.

"Yes. I still talk to her from time to time. She also told me you got engaged recently. Although I guess you aren't anymore, since you were on a first date with another guy."

In retrospect, I shouldn't have been surprised. It's been several years since Kayla and I have had an actual conversation, but we still follow each other on social media, liking each other's posts from time to time. And as her former roommate for two years, Kayla was always more Celeste's friend than mine.

I let out a quick breath to reorient myself. My thoughts

are all jumbled up together, but I start from the first thing Celeste mentioned and take it step by step. "You're right. I did block you on social media. That was childish of me, and I apologize. I was young, and I was hurting a lot, and that's the best way I could think of coping. And it's true that I moved on quickly from you, I admit that. But, Celeste, you didn't tell me you were coming back. You didn't tell me anything at all, no matter how much I reached out in the first couple of months. The only reason I even knew you were still alive is because the little '1' disappeared on KakaoTalk every time you read my messages."

Celeste's eyebrows knit together. For a moment, I think she's going to keep being mad at me. But then she takes a deep breath and exhales softly.

"I'm sorry I ghosted you," she finally says. "The first few months back were hell for me. My emotions were all over the place, and I was in so much pain that I lashed out at the people who loved me the most. It was to the point that my best friend in Seoul almost disowned me. Luckily, he didn't, but I didn't want to say the wrong thing and accidentally hurt *you*, too. In retrospect, I should have just said something simple like 'Hi, I'm still alive. Will reach out later.' Hindsight is a bitch. Other than that, well, I naively assumed..."

She trails off and downs the remainder of her beer.

"Assumed what?"

"It sounds so silly now, but I thought a few months wouldn't be that big of a deal, since we promised we'd spend the rest of our lives together."

My heart sinks. I almost want to stop Celeste from telling the rest of her story. But I don't, because I need to hear this. I need to hear her side of what happened eight years ago.

"When things finally got better around April," Celeste continues, "I felt weird replying to messages you'd left me months ago on KakaoTalk. So I tried to DM you on Instagram instead, but I discovered you'd blocked me. I reached out to Kayla, and that's how I found out about you and James. It... absolutely *broke* me."

Tears spring to her eyes, as if the memory alone is too much to bear.

My gut twists. Every excruciating emotion ranging from sadness to remorse rushes inside me.

All things considered, I don't regret jumping into a relationship with James. I wouldn't be who I am—*where* I am—without the choices I made in the last eight years. If I hadn't moved up to San Francisco, I would have never met Val or Kiara, two friends I can't even imagine my life without now. I would have never met Evelyn or any of my coworkers at *Horizon*. But I do wish things between Celeste and me hadn't happened the way they did.

I regret hurting the person that was once the love of my life.

"I'm so sorry, Celeste," I reply, because that's the only thing I manage to say out loud. It's my turn to drink.

"Hey, everyone, we're the Irish Fighters!" announces the Dave Grohl look-alike onstage. "We're usually a Foo Fighters cover band, but in the spirit of the holiday season, we'll be bringing you some good ole holiday music, along with some crowd favorites that you'll probably recognize. So, sing along, be jolly, and get drunk! Happy holidays!"

Cheers erupt from all around us. Celeste wipes away her tears and relaxes her shoulders. She looks visibly grateful for the distraction.

I also try to relax and take another sip of my beer.

"Are we good now?" Celeste asks when the people around us settle down. Her gaze is softer now, even though it's still a little tense. "Or at least, good enough for us to work together? I don't know about you, but to me, it sounds like we both fucked up. I mean, our frontal lobes hadn't even fully developed yet, so I guess it's not surprising. I'm willing to put the past behind us if you are, since I know this project is important for both you and me. I'd hate for what happened *eight years ago* to get in the way of it."

Before I can even formulate a response, Fake Grohl shouts into his mic, "Let's start off with a song I *know* you all know the lyrics to! Here's 'Mr. Brightside'!"

I groan and cover my face with my hands. A burst of laughter escapes from Celeste. I look up in time to see a small, knowing smile flash across her face before it disappears. She must remember how much I hate this song—because it's so overplayed, no real offense to the Killers.

Drunken cheers fill the pub as the band plays the all-too-familiar opening riff. People start bouncing up and down, belting the lyrics and rendering all conversation impossible. A single song has somehow unified everyone at the

Irishman's Jig. Once-strangers now have their arms around each other's shoulders as they scream-sing in unison.

As much as I hate "Mr. Brightside," in this moment, I'm grateful for the song, because I have no idea how to answer Celeste's question. We're not "good," but we're no longer "bad," either. My emotions were already a jumbled mess after the last several weeks. And our conversation only made things worse.

Celeste orders another round for us, and we both down our drinks. Before I even know what's happening, she has her arm around my shoulders, loudly singing the chorus along with the rest of the pub. I roll my eyes, but I join in anyway, because of course, I've heard "Mr. Brightside" enough times to know all the lyrics. Even though I prefer "Somebody Told Me" over it any day.

The small building shakes from all the yelling. Celeste and I laugh as one drunk woman tries to stand up on one of the tables, only to be waved off by a waiter.

We get a few more songs and drinks in when suddenly, my stomach lurches. The ground spins beneath my feet, and I sit back down.

"I think I need to head home," I hear myself saying. My own voice sounds far away, like it's on the other side of a tunnel.

Celeste takes the beer glass from my hand and sets it down on the table.

"Okay," she says, "let's get you home. Where do you live?"

Even in my drunken state, I panic, realizing that if I tell

her my current address, there's a good chance that she and my friends will cross paths. Which is something I can't deal with right now.

"I don't know," I lie.

Celeste's eyes widen in concern. "You must be more drunk than I thought."

Trying to tell her I'm fine, I get out of my seat and stand up, only for the ground to come rushing toward me.

"Gem!" Celeste grabs my arm so I don't crash onto the floor. The sudden change in momentum makes me careen toward her. She grabs me before we hit each other, but not before my lips almost graze hers.

My eyes widen. Hers do, too. Celeste has gorgeous eyes, a rich, mocha brown that are several shades darker than mine.

I drop my gaze to her red-painted lips.

If I were sober, I would have pushed her away and wiped my mouth in disgust. If I were sober, I'd have even thrown salt behind my back.

But I'm not sober. And in this one moment, I *really* want to kiss Celeste.

So I do.

Celeste

When Celeste first got Gemma's email, the last thing she expected to happen was for she and her ex to be pressed against each other, lip-locked while a local band scream-sang "Jingle Bell Rock." But life's full of surprises.

Gemma's lips are warm and impossibly soft, just the way Celeste remembers them being. Even the flavor of the beer is familiar, since Blue Moon was always Gemma's favorite. Celeste is pretty sure the last time she tasted Blue Moon, it was on Gemma's lips, too.

Celeste lets the kiss go on for longer than she should, but she pulls away before their tongues can touch. Because she *is not* French-kissing her ex. Not now, not ever.

Fortunately, San Francisco is one of the gayest—if not *the* gayest—cities in America, so no one in the bar looks twice at them. But Celeste tenses up anyway, out of habit.

The consequences of growing up in a highly homophobic family.

"Gem," Celeste says. "Come on, let's go."

"Huh?" It's clear from Gemma's voice that she's definitely not all there at the moment.

Luckily, Gemma's able to sit herself back down in her chair. But she slumps forward and rests her head on the table soon after that.

Celeste sighs. In retrospect, she should have known better. Gemma was a lightweight when they last drank together, and apparently that's not something age and experience can help with. Or at least, it's not for Gemma.

Celeste can't blame Gemma for mentally checking out for the night. Although she's glad they got everything out of the way, her heart still aches from the stress of digging up the past.

Celeste wishes she could order another drink—or two. But of course, she can't, because *someone* has to make sure they get home safely. To someone's home. Probably her own. Or, at least, her Airbnb here in SF.

With Gemma so incapacitated, Celeste has no other choice.

When their rideshare driver arrives, Celeste lifts Gemma up from her chair. Luckily, Gemma's pretty petite, so she's able to princess-carry her without any issues. Why make a drunk girl walk when Celeste can carry her and avoid any more falls?

In her arms, Gemma is soft and warm in a not unpleasant way. Celeste tries her best to ignore how her own skin tingles from how close the other woman's body is pressed against hers.

On her way to the door, a lot of people, a good chunk of them drunk out of their minds, cheer them on. One guy makes a disgusting comment about "hot lesbians," and Celeste rolls her eyes. Drunk or not, he's lucky she has her hands full, because she'd have punched him otherwise. She knows she shouldn't be surprised by his perverted outburst, but she still kind of is. Some men really are the worst.

When Celeste places Gemma in the back seat and walks over to get into the other side, she gets a flashback from the last time she saw Gemma, which also included someone getting too drunk and needing an Uber home. It occurs to Celeste that she has no idea what kind of life Gemma lives now as a twenty-nine-year-old. For all she knows, getting drunk or being around drunk people is a normal part of Gemma's current lifestyle.

Her ex had never been the partying type when they were in college, only going to the occasional gathering with Celeste when their friends invited them out. So even though Celeste shouldn't care about Gemma or give a fuck about how she lives her life now, Celeste can't help but feel a bit worried. This isn't the Gemma she used to know.

As the car takes them back to her place, Celeste finally lets herself stare at her ex. Like herself, Gemma has a few more curves, sunspots, and wrinkles than she had in college. Her long hair is dyed a chestnut brown, and she does her makeup differently now, with more blush and glossy lipstick. But she's just as adorable and beautiful as Celeste remembers her being. Maybe even more.

While they were dating, Celeste joked that Gemma was the perfect combination of cute and sexy. Exactly Celeste's type. And that hasn't changed at all in the last eight years.

Just thinking about the kiss they shared not even an hour ago stirs something inside Celeste that she didn't know she still felt for Gemma. She has to force herself to look away.

Sure, they'd kissed, but there's no telling if Gemma's even interested in her that way anymore. A lot of people randomly kiss or hook up with an ex when they're drunk.

Almost on an impulse, Celeste checks Gemma's left hand. Sure enough, no ring. Just a small indentation around her finger. So the breakup was recent, then. A rush of relief—one that Celeste knows she doesn't have any right to feel—washes over her at the thought of Gemma being single again.

Just then, Celeste's phone lights up with a KakaoTalk message from Min-joon. Did you meet her?

It's in Korean, like all her messages with Min-joon and their other friends in Seoul. She's fluent in both languages, so without much effort, she switches her phone keyboard language from English to Korean to reply, Yes.

Her phone immediately lights up again, but this time with an incoming video call. Celeste immediately declines it. Not now. I'll call you back later.

As fun as it would be to tell Min-joon about what happened in the last couple of hours, it'd have to wait. Gemma, she knows, is a light sleeper. It's a miracle she hasn't woken up yet for this entire car ride.

When they arrive at her Airbnb, Celeste has to remind herself that, even though she still knows Gemma's little quirks, like her low alcohol tolerance and her sleeping habits, she and her ex are practically strangers now. It's no longer any of her business how the other woman lives her life. Or if she's single.

After tucking Gemma into her own bed and washing up for the night, Celeste makes up her mind. She has to keep her distance from her ex while they work on this project. Or at least, she has to, emotionally. Developing new feelings after all these years will not only be a distraction from the project at hand, but also probably a fool's errand.

And "Modern Love in Focus" is much too important, for both her *and* Gemma, to be ruined by drama, past or present.

Gemma

The next morning, I'm not in my own bed.

Head pounding, I jerk up to a sitting position and look down at myself. Thankfully, I'm still fully clothed, wearing yesterday's dress and makeup. *Not so* thankfully, my face feels crusty, and my mouth is dry and feels disgusting. My breath probably stinks, too.

I can't remember the last time I got this fucked up. College, maybe?

I don't have to look around much to guess where I am. It's obvious from the bright pink comforter and frilly lace pillowcases that I'm in Celeste's bed.

Even though we lived together for over a year, we kept our separate twin beds since I wasn't officially out yet and my parents lived less than an hour away—at most two, with bad traffic. They had a bad habit of "stopping by" unannounced, and we didn't want to make them suspicious whenever they visited. On a practical level, we were also, of course, two broke college students that couldn't spring for a queen.

I used to tease Celeste about how she was totally an emo goth girl who secretly had a Barbie-pink bedroom, since her bedding and curtains were all pink, even though she almost always wore black in college.

"Pink is far from my favorite color, but I still find it comforting," she'd explained one night. "Probably because my mom always bought me pink decor back at home. What can I say, I'm a creature of habit."

My heart aches with the knowledge that, despite the many years that'd passed since Celeste and I were together, some things remain the same.

I've gotten so used to sleeping on Clementine for the past couple of weeks that now, just lying in a bed feels like a forbidden luxury. The silk sheets are cool and smooth against my cheek, and after a few minutes, I reluctantly brush the blankets aside to get up from bed.

A familiar, spicy smell gently wafts to me as I approach the bedroom door.

Haejang-guk, I think, remembering the hearty cabbage and meat hangover soup I ate with my cousins when I visited them in Seoul after college graduation. When we walked into a restaurant at three a.m. after a night of clubbing, I'd been so surprised to see it almost completely full. My cousins explained it's a common custom for Koreans to eat haejang-guk at the end of a night out to help mitigate a hangover the next day.

I had fun with my cousins, but I never told them that I'd asked them to take me out because Seoul is also Celeste's hometown, and I secretly hoped to run into her.

Twenty-two-year-old me had known that Seoul is a huge city with millions of people, but she'd still been unable to let go of the naive fantasy that we'd have some miraculous K-drama moment, where I'd catch a glimpse of her on the subway or see her while crossing a busy intersection in Hongdae. Even though I'd started dating James a couple months before and was perfectly content in that relationship, I just wanted to get a glimpse of her, if only to confirm with my own eyes that she still existed after seemingly disappearing from my life forever. I didn't even want to date her at that point. I simply wanted closure.

Unsurprisingly, I didn't find her during that trip, and I figured it was for the best. When James asked me later that summer if I wanted to move in with him after we'd both accepted our respective positions at *Horizon*, I said yes, fully ready to start our new life together in San Francisco.

Of course, now I know why Celeste disappeared from my life. And I know that in the same summer I was having the time of my life with my cousins in Seoul, Celeste was going through a hell I can't even imagine.

I stumble out of the bedroom, my heart squeezing from the pain of both the past and present.

Celeste's kitchen is sleek and modern, with black countertops and a stainless-steel fridge. It's the kind of industrial aesthetic environment that suits her outfits more, which is how I know this part of the house wasn't decorated by Celeste herself. It occurs to me then that this whole place must be an Airbnb or another temporary lodging of some sort, since Celeste is only staying in the area until mid-January at the latest, our deadline to finalize everything. She probably replaced the bedding with her own. Which is a very *her* thing to do.

Celeste stands at the stove, her back to me as she cooks, stirring the big pot with a silver ladle. Everything smells so good, and the rich kimchi smell makes my mouth water.

When she hears me approach, Celeste stiffens but doesn't turn around.

"Hey," she says.

I clear my throat. There are a million things I want to ask her right now, but the question that comes out of my mouth is "Since when do you cook?"

Back in college, I used to always be the one that made our meals, while Celeste took care of the cleaning and tidying up around the apartment. I'm shocked that she's making haejang-guk from scratch, instead of ordering delivery.

"Since I had to take care of my mom when she was sick," she replies. "You learn a lot in times of desperation."

If we were still together, or even if we were still friends, I'd rush up to hug her. But since we're not, I stand there awkwardly as Celeste brings the ladle to her lips. My eyes automatically follow the movement, and before I know it, I'm staring at her lips as she tastes the soup. Damn it.

"What happened last night?" I ask.

"You don't remember?"

In Korean, instead of saying we "blacked out," we say "the film ended" to describe the unpleasant experience of not having any recollection of what happened after a night of drinking. A lot is lost to me, and the final thing I remember before waking up in Celeste's bed is...

I gasp, bringing my hand to my lips. I've been so preoccupied with memories of the distant past that I only now remember more recent events.

I fell, and Celeste and I kissed.

Celeste silently watches me, carefully studying every slight change of the expressions on my face.

"You passed out, and I brought you back to my place," she goes on when I don't say anything. "Don't worry, nothing else happened, and I slept on the couch. The stew is ready. Let's eat."

I sit down and, after waiting for Celeste to join me at the table, eat my first spoonful. The hearty stew warms me up instantly, the pleasantly spicy flavors revitalizing my senses so that after only a few spoonfuls in, I really do feel rejuvenated.

"Thanks for cooking," I say when I finish my bowl. "And for bringing me back from the pub last night. Sorry things got so...out of hand."

"No problem. I'm glad I was there to help you."

It's a sweet thing to say, but there's not a single ounce of affection or warm emotion in her voice. In fact, she looks visibly uncomfortable.

By then, the elephant in the room is unbearably obvious, so I blurt out, "We kissed."

"We kissed," she says it back matter-of-factly. "It's fine. I know it was an accident. We should avoid drinking the next time we meet up, though. And maybe focus on work."

"Right. Glad we're on the same page."

When we finish eating, she gets up to set the pot on the stove to cool off, and I take our spoons and now empty bowls and put them in the sink. It's purely out of habit, since back at my friends' apartment, I always help them clean up after a meal. So I don't think about what I'm doing until Celeste stiffens.

"You could have just left everything on the table," she says. "Thanks, though."

A strained look crosses her face. And it's only then that I realize how familiar this all is. Eating breakfast with Celeste and cleaning up together afterward.

I get a flashback of how Celeste's hair looked first thing in the morning, messy yet still beautiful with the sunlight streaming in from the pink curtains of our bedroom. I remember all the hearts she drew while we ate our meals—either with ketchup or with gochujang, depending on whether we were eating American or Korean food. And I remember how we laughed almost every day we were together, often because we saw something funny on the internet or at school, but mostly because we just really liked being around each other.

The Celeste of today, cool and indifferent, might as well be a whole other person. And in a way, she is.

I back away from the kitchen. "I should get going. Thanks again for everything."

Celeste's eyebrows knit together, but she smiles politely, nevertheless. "No problem," she says. "Get home safe."

A quick Google Maps search tells me Celeste's place is in Nob Hill and only a couple minutes' walk from a cable car stop. I rarely ride cable cars, but since it's the fastest way to the N Muni line, I end up riding one with a group of excited tourists. It's a nice change of pace, and the happy squeals of kids as we go down the hills bring a smile to my face.

Even so, I don't let myself fully relax until I'm on the Muni back to my friends' apartment. The train car is full of people going about their Saturday around the city. Everyone is high energy today, like the college students in cosplay chatting loudly as they head to an anime convention or the little kids bouncing up and down in their seats.

And then there's me, slumped over on my seat and resting my forehead on the cool glass of the train window. Somehow, I'm on the Muni Ride of Shame again, this time for a wholly different reason than I was last month.

Clearly, when it comes to Celeste, I can't trust myself to make good choices.

By the time the train gets to my stop, I resolve to tell Val and Kiara everything.

Gemma

Since the front door opens into the kitchen, I'm hit with the buttery smell of freshly made pancakes as soon as I slip inside my friends' apartment. Val's at the stove, singing along at the top of her lungs in Spanish to Fuerza Regida as she cooks breakfast, holding the spatula like a mic. She must have not heard me come in, because she doesn't turn around.

For a moment, I stand there with my back against the door, watching my friend as she prepares two steaming hot plates of scrambled eggs, bacon, and chocolate chip pancakes.

Val and Kiara have a cute tradition where they—well, mostly Val—make a home-cooked breakfast every Saturday morning, a sacred ritual that goes back to the first time Kiara slept over. Val claims that that's how she "got the girl," because during that fateful meal, she promised Kiara that she would make the same breakfast for her every Saturday as long as they both lived.

I think about sneaking past Val, but then I spot a pancake currently cooking—*smoking*—on the pan. It's dangerously close to being burnt.

"Need help?" I finally ask. "That pancake looks ready."

Val startles, but then expertly flips the pancake before turning around to look me up and down. She lowers the volume of the music before saying, "So you're alive after all."

"Is Gemma back?" Kiara walks into the kitchen, holding Burrito. "Not to sound like an overprotective parent, but where were you last night, Gemma? You could have at least sent a text or something. Even the Financial District isn't as safe as it seems. One time, a friend of mine got mugged there in broad daylight!"

Burrito lets out a small yowl of protest, and Kiara places him on the floor. He makes a beeline for his bowls, and after a few licks of water, he comes over to weave between my legs, purring.

I sigh. "Sorry," I say to my friends, not the cat. "My phone must have died after I got shitfaced."

"With *who*?" Val and Kiara ask in unison.

I reach down to scratch Burrito in between his ears. He closes his eyes and lies down on the floor, enjoying the attention.

"It's a long story," I say. "I'll tell you over breakfast? I already ate, so no need to make me a plate, by the way."

"You sure you don't want a chocolate chip pancake?" Val asks as she hands Kiara her plate. "We have extra."

I eye the pancake. I'm still full, but the gooey chocolate chips *do* look good. "Okay, thanks. I'll take one."

"No problem, I got you!" Val smiles. "Go lock up Burrito and sit down with Kiara at the dining table."

I carefully pick up Burrito from the floor. He lets out a small, indignant mew.

"Don't worry, kitty cat," I say. "I'll bust you out of the room as soon as we're done eating."

As cute as Burrito is, he has a very naughty habit of stealing human food. Whenever we lock him up, he instantly goes from being "a manly, absolute unit" of a cat—Val's words, of course—to, as Kiara says, "just a baby!" Puss in Boots wide eyes and all. I try my best to ignore his sad little mews as I put him in the bedroom.

After I close the door behind me, I join Kiara at the dining room table. Val comes soon after with our plates and exits out of the music streaming app on her PS5. She sits down at the head of the table. Kiara sits at her right, while I sit at her left. It's the same seating arrangement we've been following for the last month or so, and it's been pretty great. Especially now that I'm paying my share of the rent—I Venmo'ed Val and Kiara while I was back in Irvine—my friends' apartment feels like a second home now.

When we're all settled, my friends wordlessly turn to me with expectant faces.

I take a deep breath and finally say, "I was with Celeste."

"Your ex?" Kiara asks, while Val says, "I thought she was in Korea!"

"She apparently moved back to LA a while ago," I reply. "Which, I had no idea about until now."

"But how did you run into her here in SF, of all places?" Val asks.

"Apparently she goes back and forth between the two cities a lot for jobs. Remember that photographer from my school? The one *Horizon* hired for the Valentine's Day issue?"

Kiara gasps. "*No.*"

"Yup. It turned out to be her."

Kiara shrieks, and Val gives me a pleased smirk.

"This is basically destiny!" Kiara says. "A match made in heaven by Sappho herself. When can we meet her? We can go on double dates!"

I fling out my hands in front of me before she can go on. This is exactly why I didn't tell my friends about Celeste sooner. The last time I saw Kiara this excited was when Val surprised her with tickets to go see Megan Thee Stallion for her birthday.

"Whoa, whoa, whoa," I say. "Just because we're working together doesn't mean we're going to date. She disappeared on me for eight years. And even if we *were* still interested in each other... we have to keep things professional for work."

Val gives me a much-deserved eyebrow raise. "Professional? Is that why you got shitfaced with her?"

I sigh. "I know, I know. I wanted to set clear boundaries and expectations. But that meant we had to talk about the past... and then I got so stressed out, I got blackout drunk for the first time in years! Which is why I stayed over at her place afterward."

Kiara looks like she's about to scream again, so I quickly add, "*But* she slept on the couch. She did make me Korean hangover soup for breakfast but—"

"*She made you breakfast!*" Kiara gestures at our now lukewarm plates of food, and I realize it's game over. Nothing I say now will convince her that Celeste and I will never date again, because to Kiara, breakfast equals love. And I guess in a way, that's true for her and Val and probably many other couples, too. But not when it comes to me and Celeste.

"Well, I'm surprised you even came back home today," Val says with a laugh.

"What do you mean?"

"You know what they say about lesbians and U-Hauls."

At my confused expression, she goes on, "Come on, you know, that one stereotype about how us sapphics move so fast in relationships that we move in together after the second date or something? Which, I mean, isn't exactly wrong considering..."

She gives a pointed look in Kiara's direction, and we all laugh.

"Oops," Kiara says with a grin. "Sorry not sorry."

Val gives her a light peck on the cheek before taking a bite out of her eggs. "Shit," she says, "the food is already cold."

"Sorry," I say. "I had a lot to catch you guys up on."

"Don't apologize for that," Kiara replies, waving me off. "We can reheat everything."

We form an assembly line from the table to the microwave,

with Kiara handing each plate of food to me and me handing it off to Val so she can reheat it. As I wait for the food to warm up, I recall how baffled I'd been when, just a week after the three of us had met for the first time at the company mixer, Kiara and Val told me that they were dating. By the end of that same month, Kiara had posted on socials that she was looking for someone to sublease her room in her apartment so she could go live with Val, her new girlfriend.

I thought it was my friends being their usual, spontaneous selves. I didn't realize there was a whole stereotype behind it. Celeste and I jumped over all that by being roommates to begin with. For better or worse.

"The U-Haul thing..." I say when we sit back down at the table with our now hot plates of food. "It worked for you guys, but Celeste and I are different. Not only did we *start* out as roommates, but she *still* ended up leaving me in the end."

Kiara squeezes my hand, and Val frowns.

"Maybe you need to establish firmer boundaries with her then," Val says, a protective edge in her voice. "So something like that doesn't happen again."

"Yup," I reply. "I think that's what I have to do, too."

I feel like I've brought everyone's mood down, because after we finish eating, my friends and I just sit there for a few awkward minutes.

Finally, I say, "You know what? We should go out tonight. Not to a bar like last time but, like, actual clubbing. It's a Saturday! I won't drink this time around, though. Since I need to take a break after last night."

My friends stare at me with expressions that say, *Are you for real?* Although Kiara, Val, and I went out a couple times when we first all became friends, we eventually stopped going out together as a group. I'm kind of to blame, since initially, it was because I was too busy doing other stuff with James. But then, as we reached our late twenties, Val and I stopped going to clubs altogether, opting for more chill activities, instead. Kiara sometimes still went out, but with her other friends.

"Gemma," Val says. "I don't know if you realize this, but we're all turning thirty next year."

Kiara holds up a hand. "For the record, *I* still occasionally go clubbing and see people older than us out and having fun all the time. But Gemma, baby, are you sure? No offense, but when's the last time you even stepped into a club?"

My face turns red. Honestly, I don't even want to do the math.

"It'll be fun!" I say, dodging her question. "Or at the very least memorable. Come on, guys. Before we get any older. Like Val said, thirty is just around the corner!"

Kiara and Val exchange a look. Kiara is practically bouncing up and down at the very prospect of clubbing with the two of us, but Val glances longingly at her PS5 as she says, "You two go ahead. My club days are over."

"Oh, come on, Valentina!" Kiara says, using her girlfriend's full first name. She grabs her arm and pulls her toward her. "You can game any night you want. Come out with us! It's not every day that *Gemma* wants to go clubbing. Or that we can all go out together!"

I give Val a pleading look. She rolls her eyes and sighs. "Fine, I'll go out. But I am *not* dressing up."

That night, after my friends pregame with some shots of tequila and I drink a glass of sparkling cider, I realize that I don't have anything to wear to the club. I left most of my clothes at James's, and I'm probably never going to get them back because I don't want to talk to him ever again. But even if I still had everything, I doubt the clubbing dresses from my early twenties fit me now—thank you, slower metabolism.

Val's closer to me in terms of size, but since she doesn't have any dresses, I end up having to borrow from Kiara. She's a few inches taller and has a totally different body type than me, but luckily she has a plain, loose-fitting black dress that doesn't look too bad on me. Meanwhile, Kiara herself wears a stunning white dress that accentuates all her curves, while Val wears an oversized black T-shirt and jeans. Like she warned us, Val doesn't dress up, but she does style her hair, slicking it back in a way that makes Kiara smile.

When we're all ready to go, we get a car and head downtown. Even though I didn't drink any alcohol, the sheer excitement of going to a club for the first time in a while with my friends sends a thrill down my spine. The lights of the city are blindingly bright, and as sirens erupt from a distance, I open the car window to feel the cool, salty San Francisco night air on my face.

That's the one thing that I like more about San Francisco than back home in Orange County. The air. Although we also have coastal areas in Southern California, up here, the cool air is so crisp and fresh in a way it never gets in Irvine.

As we approach our destination, the streets get more and more crowded with people headed out for a good time. It's eleven p.m. on a Saturday, and the city is very much alive.

Inside the club, loud EDM bombards my senses, making every cell in my body vibrate. Everything's lit up by floor-to-ceiling lights that flash and pulse to the music. Bright splashes of color shine over the entire room as throngs of people scream, laugh, and dance. The vibes and energy are so top-notch, I'm ecstatic. And I can tell my friends are excited to be here, too. Kiara is grinning from ear to ear, and even Val nods and pumps her fist along to the beat.

"Come on," I say, leading my friends to the dance floor. "Let's get closer to the stage!"

The crowd gradually makes way for us as we push closer to the front. I definitely haven't missed the stench of sweaty bodies, but being in close proximity to so many other people makes me feel alive in ways I can't explain. Kiara and I dance back-to-back, reaching our hands high in the air, while beside us, Val rocks and grooves to the music.

The club crowd is a lot younger than I remember it being, although I see a handful of middle-aged couples as well. Kiara was right. There *are* lots of people who are older than us, including a man in his seventies sporting a fedora and sunglasses. So I don't feel *too* old.

The DJ puts on a remixed version of Rihanna's "Only Girl (in the World)," a throwback from when I was in high school that makes people hoot in recognition. I close my eyes and raise my hands as I sway from side to side.

Kiara and I sing along to the lyrics, throwing Val a pointed look.

"Come on!" I say. "I know you know the words!"

Val rolls her eyes in mock disgust. But at the next chorus, she belts out the song with so much force that Kiara and I fall into each other, nearly collapsing with laughter.

Fuck, this is fun, I think. *Why did I stop going out with my friends, again?*

But of course, I know exactly why. When James and I first moved to San Francisco, we went out to pretty much every club we could get into. But as we got older, we started doing what *he* said were more "normal" mid-to-late-twenties activities like trivia nights and wineries. Since I did enjoy most of the things we did together, I never really complained.

Now, as I'm dancing in the middle of the dance floor with my friends, I realize that what James said was a "normal transition" isn't normal at all. At least, it wasn't for me. The heart-pumping music... flashing strobe lights... I still love all these things now, as much as I did in my early twenties. *This* is who I am. Not board games and escape rooms.

I resent James. But if I'm being honest, I resent my past self, too. Why didn't I speak up for myself more? Why did I let a man dictate what I should or shouldn't do? He still randomly decided he didn't love me anymore and replaced me with a Victoria's Secret model look-alike.

Never again, I think. *Fuck men!*

We're now all bouncing to a more recent EDM song with a hammering beat. The music crescendos, and the DJ throws up his arms. Smoke blows up into the air, and I'm momentarily blinded by lasers as confetti rains down from the ceiling.

Kiara and Val cheer, and I scream, for the first time in ages, with unreserved delight.

12

Gemma

On Monday morning, Evelyn asks me to come into her office.

"We've managed to secure two couples for the first set of interviews," she says when I walk in. "With Christmas coming up in a couple weeks, it'd be great if you and Celeste could interview them and submit everything by the next Monday, before the holiday. Things will get undoubtedly tricky to schedule around Christmas, but like I mentioned in my emails, we should be fine as long as we finish all the interviews by mid-January so we can take the rest of the time to edit and transmit for the print edition. Also..."

I tense up. "Also?"

Evelyn glances around and lowers her voice. "It's not one hundred percent confirmed yet, but Citrine is talking about making 'Modern Love in Focus' the cover story for the February issue. They just want to see a draft or two from you and Celeste before they make the final decision."

My skin buzzes with excitement. My first cover story after seven years of working for the magazine. This is huge.

Back when James and I lived together, we had a stack of printed *Horizon* issues with his cover stories—because luxury real estate, his focus, apparently brought in more print sales. Meanwhile, most of my work has appeared in the digital edition only, since the magazine only prints stories that the higher-ups believe will be the most profitable.

"By the way," Evelyn continues. "Speaking of Celeste, you've met up with her already, right? Just to make sure you two are on the same page?"

Oh, we've met up all right.

"Yes," I say. That's the most I can say without giving away anything in my voice.

"And it wasn't too . . . awkward?"

I grit my teeth and give Evelyn a forced smile.

"Ah." She raises her eyebrows at me. "Well. Thank you for being willing to work with her. I'll email you all the details shortly so you can set things up for the first two interviews."

"Got it, thanks, Evelyn."

Back at my desk, I read over her email with all the logistics. Most of it is straightforward, and the hardest part is going to be conveying all this information to Celeste.

I start composing a new email message.

From: gemmacho@citrine.com
To: celestemin@celestemin.com
Subject: First Set of Interviews

Hi, Celeste. Sorry again about what happened over the weekend. We got our first set of interviews . . .

I stop. I'm being too casual. Since I don't know how private our work emails are, I can't risk sounding so suspicious.

I delete everything and try again.

From: gemmacho@citrine.com
To: celestemin@celestemin.com
Subject: First Set of Interviews

Hi, Celeste. We got our first set of interview assignments. See the below forwarded message from Evelyn for more info. Are you available to do the first set of interviews this week?

Best,
Gem

I delete and rewrite a few sentences. I groan, wondering if I'll ever be able to communicate normally with Celeste again.

I'm so preoccupied by my predicament that I only realize

I wrote "Gem" and not "Gemma" *after* I hit send. I don't get much time to dwell on it, though, because Celeste's response comes in five minutes.

From: celestemin@celestemin.com
To: gemmacho@citrine.com
Subject: RE: First Set of Interviews

Yes.

-C

I let out a breath, simultaneously relieved and disappointed by her response. On one hand, since we're communicating via email, I'm glad Celeste is being succinct and professional. But it also feels weird, especially after what happened last weekend.

I play along, anyway.

From: gemmacho@citrine.com
To: celestemin@celestemin.com
Subject: RE: RE: First Set of Interviews

Great, I'll reach out to the couples we're interviewing and see what times work best for them.

I woke up in her bed this past weekend, and now she's barely saying anything in response to my emails, I think.

I let out a small, exasperated laugh before I hit send.

~

Because the first group consists of college students, both the couples we're interviewing ask if we can do Friday afternoon, after they get out of their classes for the week. It's a little tight, but I make it happen.

Luckily, Celeste's rented studio is close to our office. It's in the Mission District, away from the tall skyscrapers and surrounded by colorful murals, trendy restaurants, and fancy bakeries.

When I follow Celeste's emailed directions to the third floor of the building, I'm instantly hit with bright light streaming through the floor-to-ceiling windows. The studio is compact yet efficient, with a large open space and a small kitchen near a red-painted staircase. Celeste's lights, stands, and other equipment are currently set up in the main area, and there's also a pink tufted sofa for the guests and a sleek white armchair by the cameras for me.

"Hey."

Celeste comes down the stairs. A high-end DSLR hangs from her neck, and she's wearing what I know is her usual studio outfit: black cargo pants and a plain white T-shirt. It's a simple enough outfit, but with the tattoos snaking down her arms, red lipstick, and hair tied back in a perfectly messy bun, she looks breathtakingly artistic and sexy, all at once.

"Hi" is all I manage to say.

She walks ahead of me and holds up one of the audio equipment sets she has laid out on the kitchen table.

"Here, I'll get you set up."

Her fingers brush against my bare skin as she mikes me up. I shiver, and not because I'm cold. In fact, I'm suddenly quite the opposite.

Thankfully, the studio door opens, and our first pair, a young white couple wearing matching University of San Francisco sweatshirts, walks in holding hands. Even without the college paraphernalia, both the girl and the guy give off an awkward, nervous energy that makes it obvious they're in their early twenties, at most.

I wonder if I was also this squirrelly in college, but then I remember the old photo I'd found on Celeste's Instagram. Yes, yes I was.

"Hi! I'm Sarah, she/her," says the girl. "Sorry, I hope it's okay that we're early. We got out of class sooner than we thought we would."

"Hey," I reply. "No problem at all. I'm Gemma Cho from *Horizon Magazine*. She/her. Thank you so much for agreeing to do this interview."

"For sure," the guy replies. "My name is Will, he/him. It's nice to meet you."

I shake both their hands.

Compared to how icy Celeste was with me, she's five times warmer—and even *bubbly*—with the students as she introduces herself and mikes them up.

"I'll be recording this interview with my video cameras over there," she says, pointing at the two cameras she has set up in different angles. "While also occasionally snapping photos with this." She holds up the camera hanging from her neck. "At any given moment, I might be moving around to check on the video cameras or to take photos, so please try your best to ignore me. We're not doing any photos or videos of people looking directly at the cameras, so do your best not to glance over. Thank you so much!"

Will and Sarah nervously look at each other and nod.

The first interview goes as well as it could. As Celeste quietly walks around behind the cameras, I ask them about how they met (a science GE class during their first year), how they defined the relationship (he asked her to be his girlfriend during a date at the Rose Garden in Golden Gate Park), and their biggest struggles (communication and making time for one another despite their challenging academic and internship loads). Even though they're young, I also ask them about their advice for other couples (don't assume that the other person can read your mind) and their hopes and future plans (to get married after graduation and get jobs close to one another).

I wrap up by asking them one last question: "How do you define love?"

Sarah and Will look at each other, their gazes growing soft.

"The warm sunlight after a cold winter," Sarah says.

"Wow," Will says, genuinely impressed. "See, you can tell she's an English major, because that was beautiful. I'm not as good with words, but I will say this. For me, love is Sarah. No one and nothing else."

"Aw!" Sarah exclaims. "That's so sweet!"

The two of them make me nostalgic about college, a

relatively simple time where my biggest problems were passing a midterm or a final. And of course, a girl named Celeste, who was once the most important person in my life before she seemingly vanished into thin air.

Well, the latter is still one of my problems.

The next couple we have scheduled for the day is queer, with Shriya, a desi lesbian girl, and Case, a nonbinary East Asian individual. Shriya has long, dark hair that directly contrasts with Case's buzz cut, which is dyed in all shades of the rainbow. Unlike the first couple, they're not dressed in any college paraphernalia, but they still have the same nervous, youthful energy.

After Celeste gets them set up, I ask them the same questions I asked the first couple. Their answers start similarly to the previous ones, but things diverge when we get to the question about struggles.

"Honestly the biggest challenge for me in terms of our relationship was trying to figure out if they were into me as more than a friend in the first place," says Shriya. "I didn't even know they were into girls."

"And I didn't know she was into nonbinary people like me," Case responds with a laugh. "I think what's also hard is people often think we're just two friends, instead of a romantic couple."

"My family also still thinks Case is a girl, even though I've told them multiple times that they're not," Shriya adds. "It's always a struggle whenever I go back home."

When I ask them about their future plans, Case says, "We have no idea how our future will look. Ideally, we'll stay here since SF is a nice little bubble apart from the rest of the country. I grew up in the Midwest, and it's so different there."

"Yeah, I'm figuring things out, too," says Shriya. "Hopefully we'll have a better idea when we start applying for jobs."

They both look at each other and smile in a hopeful way that's so sweet and familiar, it almost makes me sick.

"One last question," I say. "How do you two define love?"

"Home," Shriya says. "You know that saying, home can be another person? Well, that's the case with me and Case. We accept each other unconditionally, like no one else has ever accepted us."

"Damn," says Case. "Definitely that! But also...shit. I don't have anything substantial to add—wait, I know! Love is being there for each other, no matter what. Ah, sorry, that's such a stereotypical answer."

Shriya shrugs. "But it's so true, though. Like, it's not just having a crush or thinking someone is hot. It's sticking together, through thick or thin."

The sun is on the verge of setting by the time Shriya and Case leave. I stay behind to help Celeste pack up her equipment. And to hopefully thaw some of the ice between us. I want to keep things professional, but that doesn't mean I want us to be so stiff and uncomfortable around each other.

The warm, cozy vibe of the studio is now gone, the waning light casting long shadows across the large open space. Everything takes on an almost haunted quality in the growing darkness, and Celeste turns on the overhead lights.

She has her back toward me, unplugging and wrapping wires around the studio, when I say, "What did you think about today's interviews?"

"They were cute," she replies. "Idealistic and naive, for sure, though. It reminded me of..."

She trails off and meets my eyes, glancing up at me from underneath her long, dark lashes. Just her looking at me like that is enough to make me warm up in places I shouldn't even be thinking of right now.

"Yeah," I say. "It made me think of us, too."

I'd only meant to engage in friendly conversation, but it's like there's no middle ground between Celeste and me. One moment, there's a big wall between us, and the next, my heart's racing and about to burst.

Celeste takes a step toward me, before clearing her throat and turning away. "So, I'll see you at the next shoot?"

"Actually," I say. "I was wondering if you wanted to meet up sometime this weekend. With how important this project is, I could use your input as I work on the write-up. For this first one, at least. Just to make sure we're on the same page about everything. And there's a couple other things I want to talk about, too. Stuff related to work, of course."

Celeste cocks her head to the side. A faint smile plays on her lips as she replies, "As long as it's not anywhere that has alcohol."

"Yeah no, of course," I quickly say. "Let's go somewhere that's the complete opposite of a bar. Like a coffeehouse."

"Sounds good. I'm free on Sunday."

13

Celeste

Celeste doesn't let herself relax until her ex leaves the studio. Gemma's honey-brown eyes, her flushed cheeks... it took all of Celeste's self-control to not close the distance between them, to not gently cup Gemma's adorably sweet face with her hands and kiss her soft pink lips.

Last Friday could have been a fluke. They both drank a lot, and Gemma especially had been drunk out of her mind. But today, they were completely sober. And Gemma had still looked at her like she wanted to devour her.

And Celeste has no idea what to do with that information.

Gemma is still physically attracted to her. So what? Gemma couldn't keep her hands off Celeste eight years ago, either, but she still started dating someone else a few months after Celeste left the country. And then moved in with him, just like that.

She'd consider asking Gemma to be friends with benefits, but they weren't even *friends* anymore. Not really. And Gemma doesn't do casual. Or at least, she didn't when Celeste knew her eight years ago.

Last week, when she'd finally told him about everything that'd been going on, Min-joon had asked, "Are you going to be okay?"

And at the time, she'd shrugged and said yes. When she agreed to stay on the project, even if that meant she had to work with her ex, it hadn't seemed like that big a deal. Eight years was a long time. And since Gemma had clearly moved on from her, Celeste thought she could keep things professional and treat this like any of her other projects.

But now . . . the lines are torturously blurry. And today's interviews were only the first set of three that Celeste has to work on with Gemma. Somehow, they have to get through two more sessions—and whatever communication and meetups needed in between—before mid-January, when she'll be free to go back to LA and resume her far less confusing life without her ex.

Before she leaves the studio, Celeste pops into the restroom upstairs to wash her face with ice-cold water. In the mirror, she looks pale, almost like a vampire with her bloodred lips and dark circles. She'd done her best to cover up her exhaustion with makeup, but now, at the end of the day, her face looks haggard, and there's visible stress wrinkles around her eyes. She hadn't been able to get much sleep ever since she first ran into Gemma at the bar, back when she was with Gretchen.

Celeste gets out her phone and goes to the conversation she has with her most recent ex, where the last sent text was Gretchen inviting her out for "the best pumpkin spice cocktails in the city." Celeste had eagerly thumbs-upped the message, since she loves seasonal drinks of any kind. And without much thought, she'd naively gone to the address the other woman had shared, excited to have a good time.

If she'd known it'd be an ambush where Gretchen would accuse her of leading her on, even though Celeste very clearly told her from the very beginning she only does casual, she never would have gone. Especially not if she'd known she'd run into her college ex.

As her thoughts wander back to Gemma, Celeste pauses. Does she really regret running into Gemma, though? Sure, it's been a hell of a lot awkward to see her again, but when she really thinks about it, it's also been kind of nice. Although it was fucking painful when they were doing it, now that they've talked about the past and apologized to each other, she's been feeling substantially lighter.

But still, Celeste reminds herself, that doesn't mean she should fully let her guard down.

She taps her phone screen and deletes the conversation she had with Gretchen. That's the problem with friends with benefits. A lot of times, people catch feelings, whether they want to or not.

14

Gemma

I spend most of Saturday visiting apartments and shared houses, but almost all of them are either out of my budget (with all the hidden fees included), a public health concern, or have roommates or neighbors that I'm not too sure about.

By the time I return to my friends' apartment at the end of the day, I'm exhausted.

Maybe I should keep living with Val and Kiara, I think.

Val had mentioned the other night the real possibility of us all getting a bigger apartment together when their lease ends in the spring, so I could have my own room and Val and Kiara could have theirs. After today, it sounds like the dream, but I also don't want to push it. My friends—and Burrito—love their current apartment. They've been here for the last several years. I don't want them to change where they live because of me.

That evening, I'm sitting side by side on Clementine with Val, going through emails and drafting some write-ups while she plays *Elden Ring*. Luckily, I'm good at blocking out background noise as I work, or else I wouldn't be able to get anything done amid the deafening music, screams, and crashing sounds coming from the TV.

Kiara's out having dinner with some of her other friends, so it's just Val and me tonight. Rather than cook for only the two of us, we decided to share a box of pepperoni pizza.

Burrito's nowhere in sight. After stealing a few pieces of crust, he sped into my friends' room, probably hiding underneath the bed from all the loud noises.

I'm about to shut my laptop and call it a night, when I get an email from Celeste. Or at least, what I think still counts as an email. There's no subject, nor a message in the body. The only thing she's included are the files for the video recordings from Friday.

"What did you *do*?" Val asks as she peers at my computer screen.

I look up to see the bloodred words YOU DIED flash across the TV. I'm not sure whether I should be honored or horrified that Val commented on Celeste's email *while* her character was getting mauled by a two-headed dragon.

Val exits out to the main menu and gives me a questioning look.

I sigh. "Things have been weird after I woke up at her place," I say. "She's being distant, which would be fine, since we have to keep things professional for work, anyway…if it weren't for the fact that she's being *so* distant that working together has become kind of uncomfortable. I tried to make things friendly between us yesterday, but then, there was this weird tension between us. I think we both still like each other?"

Val gasps and sets her controller down on the coffee table. "Wait, isn't that a good thing, though? Kiara's sapphic shipping fantasy is coming true."

I lean back into Clementine's soft upholstery. "I don't know if I want to get into all that right now."

"What, because of work?" Val resumes her game, and after watching her character dodge around and hack at the dragon for several minutes, I'm convinced she's forgotten about our conversation, when she says, "Don't you think Kiara is right, even just a little bit? Don't get me wrong. I'm not superstitious or even a little -stitious. Not the slightest. But you crossed each other's paths after *eight years*. When most exes from high school or college don't ever see each other again."

Hack, hack, dodge, slash.

I watch the screen as she speaks, mesmerized by the deft way she's making her character move around and attack the dragon as she continues, "I don't know about you, but fuck work. If I were you, I'd at least try to see if there's still something there between us."

I shake my head. "I can't 'fuck work,' though. This is quite literally the most important project I've ever had at *Horizon*."

"Fine." *Slash, dodge, roll, slash.* "Then get all your work done *and then* fuck."

A startled guffaw of laughter escapes from my lips. I love how little a filter Val has. I always have.

"You know, sometimes, dating is like playing a challenging game like *Elden Ring*," she continues, gesturing at the screen with her controller. "Once you get going, you can't hit pause. It's full of surprises, and you'll make a lot of mistakes before you get better."

Celeste and I are nowhere near the possibility of dating again. But I listen to my friend anyway, since I know she's trying to help. Plus, it's absolutely amazing how Val's managing to skillfully attack the monster on-screen while keeping up our conversation.

Stab, dodge, stab, stab.

"For much of it," Val continues, "you'll have no idea what the fuck you're doing or if what you're doing is even worth it. But trust me, when things are good, you'll get the biggest rush of euphoria you can legally get."

I scoff, finally looking away from the TV. "As if you and Kiara ever struggle that much with each other."

Still keeping her eyes glued to the screen, Val raises her eyebrows. "Are you kidding me? Of course we do. Why do you think she's out with her friends right now?"

My eyes widen. "Did you guys fight while I was out today?"

She somehow manages to shake her head while mashing a bunch of buttons.

"No, not today. But we used to a lot more when she first moved into my place. Once we started to officially live together, Kiara and I realized we're completely different people. She's an extrovert who loves to hang out with a lot of different people and wants to go out every day, while I'm content to play video games after work and meet my friends virtually. You're one of my only friends that I regularly go out to meet in real life. And you don't even count as that anymore, since we live together now."

I blink. "Wow, really? I'm honored."

"You should be. Anyway, so at first Kiara and I thought the solution was to take turns doing what the other person liked to do. Some weekends I would go out with her, and others she'd stay in and play video games with me. It worked at first, but then we were both so stubborn about getting each other to try what we ourselves liked to do that, in the end, we became burnt out. And resentful. Eventually, things got so bad that we started to think we weren't compatible enough and thought about breaking up."

"Wait, what?" I ask. "When was this? Why didn't I hear about this happening? Or almost happening?"

My heart twists just hearing about the possibility of my friends breaking up. It's shocking to hear that Kiara and Val suffered from the same problem that James and I eventually did, after the initial rush of feelings and excitement faded away and we realized we were two different people. Of course, now, though, I know my way of going about things was totally wrong. Because I thought I could keep the peace by letting him completely steamroll me.

I'm more than a little curious as to how my friends got through it.

"Like, a little over five years ago?" Val replies. "Around Christmastime. Granted, we still fight from time to time, but that was our biggest argument, I think."

Five Christmases ago, I was out of town for a ski trip in Aspen with James's family, having what was then one of the best Christmases I ever had in my entire life. It was during a time when things were amazing between James and me, when our relationship was still relatively new and fun, and, aside from weekday lunches with my friends at work, I admittedly didn't talk at length with anyone except him on a day-to-day basis.

That was so extremely unhealthy, I think. *And selfish.*

I wish I could travel back in time and give Past Me a good shake.

Val must have sensed my guilt, because she says, "It's fine. It happens. People lose themselves in relationships all the time, especially in their early twenties. We live and we learn, right?"

"Yeah," I say softly. "Wait, so what happened?"

Val laughs, so loudly and unexpectedly that I jump. "Well, after talking through a bunch of stuff, we went back and realized the rules we established for ourselves in the beginning of our relationship were bullshit. And we learned that we need to just let each other be who we are, instead of trying to change ourselves or each other. Sure, we make sure to regularly do things together, but we've also been doing things separately ever since, and it's worked *beautifully*."

I stare down at my hands, wondering if that's where I

went wrong with James. I'd been so busy with my work at *Horizon*, giving *other* people advice or telling them about the best romantic date spots in town, that I took the back seat in my own relationship. Things were so much easier when I followed James's lead, doing whatever he wanted to do. That is, before he led our relationship into a gaping black hole.

Val jumps off the couch and lets out a big roar of triumph. "Yeah! Take that, Dragonlord Placidusax!"

Startled, I make a face, looking up at the screen in time to see the two-headed dragon disintegrate and blow away in a cloud of dust. "Is that really the dragon's name?"

"The *late* dragon's name," Val answers proudly.

Sure enough, DRAGONLORD PLACIDUSAX flashes as an achievement trophy on the TV.

Grinning widely like... well, someone that's just beaten a challenging video game level... Val sets her controller down and grabs an uneaten pizza crust.

As she eats, she glances over at my face and does a double take.

"Oh, no," she says. "You're thinking of James, aren't you? Honestly, fuck that guy. I didn't tell you all this so you'd feel bad about the past. What I wanted to say is... hell is trying to control people, including yourself. Be nicer to yourself, and let you be you, and let Celeste be herself. If you guys end up taking this further than a business relationship, great. If not, that's fine, too. Don't try to force the hand in either direction. Just be sure you know what *you* want."

At that moment, the front door unlocks and Kiara walks in, a wine-dazed smile on her face. Burrito shoots out from the bedroom, greeting her with joyful meows.

"Babe!" Val leaps up from Clementine to give Kiara a big hug.

"Aw, babies!" Kiara scoops up Burrito and squeezes Val tight. "I missed you two!"

My friends kiss each other, and I grin.

If that isn't true love, I don't know what is.

Gemma

On Sunday morning, a full two hours before Celeste and I are supposed to meet, I arrive at Peter's, a nice coffeehouse that Val, Kiara, and I stop at often since it's only a five-minute walk from their place. As locations go, I figure it's the best option, since it's a brightly lit, wide-open space, pretty much the opposite of the dark and cramped places I've been meeting Celeste outside of work lately. It also has such a nice, productive vibe that I hope will help us stay on track.

It's foggy and cloudy today, and there's enough moisture in the air that I bring an umbrella in case it rains. But that doesn't deter people from being out and about. Traffic is bustling, and even from inside the coffeehouse, I can hear honking cars and sirens passing by.

I put on my earbuds and get started on work. The first thing I do is go over the footage and photos that Celeste sent me. As I review everything, I have to admit that it all works perfectly. The lighting, the angles, and the editing… Celeste managed to set up all the components of the shoot flawlessly in a way that makes everything from Case's rainbow-colored hair to even finer details like Will's dimples really shine through the cameras. And she's already edited out all the unnatural pauses and other awkward instances that occurred while the kids were speaking.

I'm finishing up the transcription of the second interview when Celeste arrives at 10:55 a.m., five minutes earlier than our scheduled meeting time. She sits down across the table from me and wordlessly watches as I type.

Before I begin a new line of dialogue, I pause the video and glance up from my screen just briefly enough to see that today, Celeste is wearing a nice white blouse with a turned-down collar and black square glasses that makes her look like a sexy schoolteacher. Intentionally or not, she's perfectly executed the hot nerd look.

"Hey," I say. "Sorry, let me finish this up before we start talking."

Celeste shrugs. "No worries. I came early."

She continues watching me work, and although I can't see her face, the knowledge that she's observing me is enough for my fingers to make typos they normally don't, like spelling "girlfriend" *girlfiend*. I clear my throat, ignoring the heat rising up in my cheeks.

"Sorry, can you not look at me while I work?" I ask. "It's distracting."

When I glance up again, Celeste's slightly widened eyes

are blinking rapidly. "Oh, sure. Sorry, I didn't think—I'm going to go get myself a coffee."

As she hastily gets up and goes to stand in line at the register, I stare at her back in confusion. What happened? Why was she so flustered?

And then, I realize. After making sure Celeste still has her back turned toward me, I look at myself in my phone's selfie camera.

Since I don't have time to think much about how I look before hopping on the Muni in the morning during weekdays, I usually throw on whatever's clean and don't even bother with anything other than sunscreen. On weekends, though, I like to dress up and wear makeup, simply because I have more time to do so.

Both times I'd last seen Celeste, I'd been wearing my usual work outfits. This is the first time Celeste has seen me in full makeup and a dress since college. Granted, there could be a whole other reason why she's acting like this. But even the slightest possibility of her becoming this worked up about me looking nicer than usual makes me blush even harder.

I barely manage to finish the transcription and hit save.

The café had almost been empty when I came in, but by the time Celeste comes back with her drink, it's almost full, probably because it's now pouring outside. Every table around us is taken with people either hanging out or just taking refuge from the rain. Friends catch up over lattes, and various individuals read books with their steaming mugs of coffee. There are even a few other people on their laptops, which makes me feel better about working on a Sunday.

Celeste sits back down, and I look up from my computer again. She's gotten herself a hot Americano in a cute turquoise mug. Yup, Celeste is definitely staring at me, her eyes lingering on my currently pink-painted lips.

I clear my throat and push my laptop in her direction. "So, what do you think? I'm going to add more text to introduce and conclude the piece when we have all the interviews, and the design team is going to make the layout look more polished, but this is basically what I have right now."

She slowly scrolls through what I have so far. From the way her eyes are moving, I can tell she's going from the pictures she took to the text I wrote and vice versa.

"It looks amazing, so far," she says. "I like the pictures you picked out. Great choices, Gem. I can tell you put a lot of care in selecting the ones you did."

"Thanks. And yeah, I did my best."

Celeste sent me a folder of all the photos she'd taken during the interviews, and it'd been up to me to choose which ones to use. It was hard to only select a few, but I tried to choose pictures that I thought best portrayed the subjects' personalities, based on the time we spent with them.

"I love this picture of Case laughing," Celeste says with a smile. "Their entire face is lighting up."

I grin, too. "Yup, that's why I chose it."

Our eyes meet. Celeste's gaze flickers down to my lips again before she looks away.

I go over some more logistical things with Celeste, explaining to her what Evelyn told me about the timeline for the project. Overall, compared to our previous encounters, it's a very productive meeting. By the time I finish, the din of the coffee shop is so loud that I have to practically shout to be heard. "Do you have any questions or concerns?"

Celeste flashes a quick, professional smile. "No," she says, also loudly. "Thanks for showing me everything. It's nice to see how it all looks put together!"

She gets up quickly, bumping right into a college student rushing to meet her friends at the door. Books and papers fly from the student's hands, along with her iced latte, which splashes all over the place. The girl's friends gasp.

"*Shit*," says Celeste.

I bend down to help the girl pick up her stuff. When I glance up again, Celeste is dabbing her chest with napkins from our table. My eyes automatically follow her hand and *holy crap*...her white shirt has gone sheer with the icy liquid, exposing the lacy bra she has underneath. I'm instantly turned on but also mortified for her. Neither of us has anything to cover her up. Since we're so close to my friends' place, I didn't bother bringing a jacket.

"Hurry up!" says one of the other students at the door. "We're going to miss the bus!"

"I'm so sorry," the girl says. "But I have to go, bye!"

The student runs to her friends, leaving Celeste and me to stare at each other. Celeste has gotten as much of the stain out as she can, which unfortunately isn't much. She wraps her arms around herself and shivers.

I don't have to look out the window to know it's still pouring outside. The rain is a steady drum that accompanies the café music, like it's part of the track.

"Did you drive here?" I try.

She shakes her head. "No. I took public transportation. Didn't want to deal with all the traffic and parking."

A quick glance tells me Celeste didn't bring an umbrella, like I did. I would just walk her to the train stop with mine, but she's already shivering now from the iced coffee. And she lives on the other side of the peninsula, so a rideshare car will not only be expensive but also take forever because of the rain and afternoon traffic.

We look at each other for a long moment, and I want to groan in frustration. This is what I get for not picking somewhere that's more in between the two of us.

"Do you want to come over to my place?" I finally ask. "It's a five minutes' walk away. I'll lend you a shirt. And maybe an umbrella, too, if it keeps raining."

Celeste raises her eyebrows. "Are you sure you'd be okay with that?"

"I can't in good conscience let you go across the city like this," I say. "Besides, I live with my friends, and they'll be home. It'll be fine."

The truth is, I have no idea whether Kiara and Val are home or not. Knowing how late they went to sleep last night after playing *Baldur's Gate 3*, I'm pretty certain they are, though.

Celeste bites her lip. "If you're sure. Thank you. I appreciate it."

When we step outside the coffeehouse, it's raining so consistently that it feels like there wasn't a time when it didn't rain.

My umbrella is small, really only meant to be used by one person. We'll have to link arms and squeeze closer together to both fit underneath. I open it and extend my arm out to her as casually as I can.

"Here," I say.

I hold my breath as she wordlessly loops her arm around mine.

At first, Celeste does her best to walk beside me, but that proves to be difficult since she's almost a head taller than me. We don't last more than a block before she has to take the umbrella from me and hold it for us instead. It's uncomfortable at first, but once we find a good way to position ourselves, it's admittedly cozy and nice, a little refuge while we walk through the cold, rainy city streets.

I hadn't accounted for how just the warmth of her body pressed against mine would make my heart race. I swallow and do my best to avoid eye contact, even as my body heats up next to hers.

"Do you remember that one time it rained really hard in LA?" Celeste asks suddenly. "It's one of the few times I remember it raining substantially while we were there for college."

"Are you talking about the time during our junior year when the entire campus was almost empty, and some professors even canceled class?"

"Yes!" Celeste laughs. "After growing up in Korea, which

has a whole *monsoon* season, I couldn't believe my ears when my professor said we should cancel class for the day because of 'rain and traffic.' "

I groan. "Oh yeah, you got to return home right away. I remember that. Meanwhile my professor stubbornly made us stay for a whole forty-five minutes and only gave up after he realized that more than half the class wasn't going to show up."

"We had fun after, though, right?" Celeste asks. "Since I made us Shin Black Ramyun, and we spent the entire rest of the day binge-watching a K-drama together."

A faint smile plays on her lips at the memory. And before I can stop myself, I'm smiling back at her.

"Yeah. You always made the best ramyun."

Although I did most of the cooking, the one thing Celeste made really well—her "signature dish," as we jokingly called it—during college was ramyun. Instead of just using the packets that came with the instant noodles, Celeste would add in a bunch of other fresh ingredients like eggs, green onions, mushrooms, and dried seaweed. We'd always eat it out of the pot with servings of kimchi in our individual bowls. It wasn't as impressive as the *haejang-guk* she made me more recently, but it was so good that I still make ramyun for myself that way out of habit, eight years later, although I'd somehow forgotten—or maybe I blocked it out—that I first learned how to do that from Celeste.

I'm so lost in thought that I don't look where I'm going, or at least not until Celeste pulls me toward her.

Whoosh. A car speeds past us, splashing water onto the back of my dress.

I'm pressed against her now, the two of us standing at the edge of the sidewalk underneath my too-small umbrella. We stay there like that for a moment that seems to stretch on for several years, my heart pounding in my chest. It's nice and warm in her arms, so much so that I can't help but linger a bit before I step away.

Her eyes still slightly widened, she says, "*Joshim-hae*," telling me to be careful in Korean. She tilts her head at my now partially wet dress. "It's a good thing you live close by."

I nod. "Guess we both got wet today."

The comment leaves my mouth before I realize how it sounds. Celeste's eyebrows shoot up before she quickly turns away so I can't see her face.

But I see her shoulders shake with silent laughter, all the same.

"Wait, so, you live with two of your friends?" Celeste asks as we walk up the stairs to the apartment. "But they're not your roommates?"

I wince. I knew this question would be unavoidable. But it doesn't make me any keener to answer it.

"Yup," I say. "Technically they *are* my roommates now, since we do live together. And I do pay my part of the rent. But I'm just sleeping on their couch until I can find my own place to live. I used to live with my ex before we broke up."

"He kicked you out?" Celeste asks. The sudden fury in her voice catches me off guard. "In what world is that fair?"

"The condo is his parents', unfortunately. And even if we had rented an apartment, I would have still been the one to move out. I can't afford to live alone in SF. He can, thanks to his family."

Celeste shakes her head. "Ah, that sucks."

"Yeah, it's okay, though. My friends have been very understanding while I get back on my feet. You'll see when you meet them. They're nice—"

I open the apartment door, only to find that no one is in the living room.

Desperation creeps into my voice.

"Hello?" I call out, hoping Val and Kiara are in their bedroom.

But no one answers. Not even Burrito. Celeste and I are completely alone.

"Fuck," I say underneath my breath.

Behind me, I hear Celeste slip into the apartment, but I don't look at her. Instead, I check my phone and see two message notifications from the group chat with my friends.

Off to take Burrito for his annual vet visit! Kiara says.

He didn't pull off a jailbreak, so don't worry, Val adds.

Both texts were received thirty minutes ago, before Celeste and I even left the coffeeshop. Only, I'd been too distracted by Celeste—and too overwhelmed—to take my eyes off her long enough to check my phone. I'm embarrassed that I hadn't even thought to look.

To her credit, Celeste doesn't say anything. She walks

past me to sit on Clementine, and I get the weird feeling of my two worlds merging, like the one I used to get as a kid when I spotted a teacher at Costco. Even though I'm the one that invited Celeste into the apartment, my brain still feels like it's short-circuiting.

Kiara and Val didn't yet exist in my life when I met Celeste. And Celeste had long disappeared by the time I'd met my friends. And yet here she is now, quietly checking her phone on Kiara's sofa. I can tell she's patiently waiting for me, too polite to comment on the awkward situation I've put us in.

I turn around and face my box of belongings so my back is to Celeste. "Let me change really quick, and then I'll find a clean shirt for you."

I grab another dress for myself and dash into the bathroom. With the door safely closed behind me, I stand with my back pressed against the wooden surface and let out a slow breath. After a few more quiet inhales and exhales, I change into the dry dress and come back out into the living room.

Celeste looks up from her phone. "Hi," she says with a small smile.

"Hi," I reply before whipping back around again.

I search through my things for a shirt that'll fit Celeste. My clothes all seem too small for her, probably since she's taller and has wider shoulders.

I know I have a bigger shirt somewhere. I just have to find it.

"Anything will do," she says after I fling a fourth shirt

behind my shoulder. "Or I can wash my shirt here and dry it if it's okay—"

"Found it!" I get up on my feet, triumphantly holding up a black, baggy T-shirt.

Celeste scoffs. "How big do you think I am?"

I hear her get up from Clementine and move toward me, but I don't realize how close she is until I accidentally back into her.

"Whoa there," she says, gently placing her hands on my arms to steady me. This is the second time today that she's touched me, and unfortunately, I still can't get enough.

I've never in my life been gladder to be wearing long sleeves, because the heat from her body is enough for my breath to catch. If we were skin to skin, I'd probably combust. Every cell in my body is aching to close the distance between us. Even though we did technically kiss back at the pub, I was too drunk to remember much of it. I want to remember this time, to fully feel every minute sensation of her lips on mine.

Snap out of it! I mentally reprimand myself.

I shove the shirt in her direction so it comes in between our bodies.

"Here," I say. "I figured you'd want a shirt you can wear without a bra, since the coffee got on it, too."

I was so one-track minded in my attentiveness that I'm wholly unprepared for how awkwardly my words hang in the space between us.

Finally, Celeste raises an eyebrow. "Oh, so you were looking at my bra?" she asks, her voice low and quiet.

She gets an intense look in her eyes, as if she's stripping me in her thoughts.

"It was kind of unavoidable," I explain. "The coffee *did* soak through your shirt."

Celeste makes a low humming sound, and my eyes drop down to her red lips. My breath hitches, and Celeste's eyes briefly flutter closed.

"Gem," she says.

Almost instinctively, I lean forward.

And then she's kissing me, rough and hard. She tosses the shirt I gave her onto Clementine before pushing me against the wall, resting an arm in a protective arch above my head. A small moan escapes from my mouth as our tongues entangle with one another, and at the sound, her eyes flutter closed with pleasure before she cups my chin with her other hand, angling my face so her tongue can press in deeper.

We stop briefly to catch our breaths before she pulls me to Clementine so we both end up on the couch, with me straddling her between my legs as we resume making out.

I unbutton the still stained but now mostly dry shirt of hers, the thing that got us into this mess in the first place. With a frustrated growl, I fling it to the ground.

Celeste's eyes widen with amusement. "What did my shirt ever do to you?" she teases, but the humor is quickly replaced by pleasure on her face as I cup her breasts, slipping my fingers under her bra to sweep over her hardened nipples.

It's almost criminal how much I missed these boobs.

"Undo my bra," she begs, and I oblige, reaching behind her to unhook the back.

The moment it drops to the floor, I'm sucking on one of her nipples while massaging the other with my fingers. She gasps, and every remaining thought leaves my brain except the need to pleasure Celeste, to touch her and make her gasp and cry out again and again.

I've just come back up to kiss her lips when behind me, someone coughs.

"Um, hi," says Val. "So, I'm assuming this is Celeste?"

Celeste's eyes widen in panic, and in one quick motion, she grabs the shirt I gave her and flings it on. Then before I can say anything, she bolts out the door, leaving me to the clutches of my best friends and their cat.

16

Gemma

Burrito lets out a little chirp of greeting before squirming out of Kiara's arms. My friends and I silently watch as he lands gracefully on the floor and starts sniffing Celeste's stained shirt. Before he can get to her bra, I swiftly pick up Celeste's things and hide them behind my back, as if that could somehow undo what were the ten most embarrassing seconds of my life.

Is this how James felt when I walked in on him and Daphne? I think. *Holy shit, is this karma?*

"And you're sure there isn't anything going on between you two?" Kiara asks with a teasing smile.

Oh, there's something going on between Celeste and me, all right. No matter how much I wish there wasn't.

"Positive," I lie.

"Why don't you toss the shirt in the laundry hamper and come talk with us?" Val asks, sounding every bit like a dad.

I do what she says. Clementine is unfortunately the only piece of furniture in the living room that can fit all three of us. So in a cruel twist of fate, my friends and I sit together on the same orange sofa where I was making out with Celeste not even five minutes ago. Thank God we'd kept most of our clothes on.

I try my best to ignore the ever-growing urge to Febreze the shit out of the couch on the off chance that it'll smell like Celeste.

"I'm so, so sorry," I say. "Everything just kind of happened. I feel horrible. You guys were nice enough to give me a place to stay while I figure things out and I completely disrespected your property. I understand if you want me to—"

Val and Kiara look at each other and burst into giggles. I'm confused, but I'm mostly relieved. Laughter is much better than the alternative.

"Gemma, you're fine," Kiara says. "I mean, it was a bit of a shock for sure, but it's not like you guys were flat out having sex in our living room or anything."

But it could have easily gone there. My face heats up, and I'm not sure from what. Shame? Arousal? All of the above?

"Still," I say. "Sorry. I lost control. It was the first time we've been that physical since college."

Val raises her eyebrows. "I wouldn't expect any less. She's the girl that made you realize you're bi, right?"

"Yeah."

My friends laugh again, and this time, I join in. From an outsider's point of view, I guess my current situation *is* funny. I can see that now that some of the embarrassment has faded away.

"So...what are you going to do now, Gemma?" Kiara asks, her voice gentle and careful.

I check my phone. Celeste and I don't text regularly. Or at least, not anymore. After what happened today, though, it feels like I should get some kind of message from her. But there's nothing. Not even a "Hey, do you have my shirt?"

"Well, if what happened today doesn't scare her off, I'll just have to keep working with her," I reply. "It's way too late to get someone else, and also, she's really good at her job."

Kiara smiles, and Val declares, "You know, I think this will be good for you. This project will help your career *and* be the perfect, hot distraction after your traumatizing breakup with James. What more can you want?"

Kiara and I make a face at her.

"Babe!" Kiara exclaims, at the same time I say, "I don't know, an actually healthy and happy relationship? A job assignment that doesn't involve working with my unfortunately sexy ex?"

Val holds out a hand. "Wait, hear me out. Are you even ready to get into another serious relationship, though? After what happened with James? I mean, come on, Gemma. It's been barely over a month, and you dated him for seven years."

Just the sound of James's name makes my jaw clench. But I see Val's point.

She takes one long good look at my thoughtful expression. "It's like what we talked about yesterday. Just have fun with it and go with the flow. Is she the type to get attached easily?"

I think back to what Celeste told Gretchen. "No, from what I've heard, she's the opposite. She doesn't do relationships anymore, apparently."

"Then that's perfect!" Val exclaims. "Come on, if James already has a sexy rebound, why can't you have one, too?"

I spend the rest of the day thinking about what Val said as I go about my usual Sunday routine of checking out apartment listings around the city, shopping for groceries, and doing laundry whenever my friends aren't using the washer or dryer. Every time I finish a task, I check my phone, hoping to see an email or a message from Celeste.

Nothing.

Since I only know her number from college and I most certainly don't want to send her an email about what happened between us today, I message her on KakaoTalk before I'm about to go to bed.

Hey, I write. Sorry about earlier. You left your shirt here. And your bra. I'll give them to you the next time we see each other.

The little "1" disappears almost instantly. For a split second, I'm afraid Celeste will ghost me like she did many years ago. But then she replies, Thanks.

I wait for her to say more, but she doesn't.

Well, I guess that's that.

Did you like it as much as I did? I type, and then delete almost immediately.

I groan, lying face down on Clementine. The orange sofa thankfully does not have to be Febrezed.

Burrito jumps up onto the couch, rubbing his head against my legs. I sit up and gently grab him, in desperate need of some cat therapy. Many head scratches and purrs later, I check my phone to see another message from Celeste.

See you later, Gem.

It's a simple enough sentence, but it's enough for me to fall asleep with a smile on my face.

~

On Monday morning, I submit everything from the first session to Evelyn for review. Evelyn responds not even fifteen minutes later with This is beautiful. Excellent work. Looking forward to seeing the others.

I send a quick message to Celeste.

Hey, Evelyn loved what we did for the first part. She said keep up the good work.

Celeste responds with a thumbs-up emoji.

And listen... I add. I'm sorry if what happened yesterday made you uncomfortable. It won't happen again, I promise.

Not even a minute after I press send, Celeste replies with Don't be. I started it.

My face heats up, like we're making out on the sofa again. I let out a quick breath and get up from my desk to grab some water. When I come back, I'm surprised to see I've received another text from Celeste.

Were your friends mad? it reads.

Oh. No? They were amused. We laughed it off.

That's good, Celeste replies. I was embarrassed.

I hesitate, and then send Celeste an emoticon of a cat gaping in surprise. I know, me too. Is that why you ran off?

Yeah.

She sends back an emoticon of a dog sweating nervously.

I grin. They were cool with it, don't worry.

Another pause. And then: Were you?

I blink and swipe at my eyes, making sure I'm reading Celeste's message correctly.

Yeah, I reply. You?

A few seconds later, Celeste says, Yeah.

I bite my lip, wondering what'll happen the next time we'll work together.

17

Celeste

On Monday night, Celeste gets an email from Gemma letting her know that their next round of interviews will be on Thursday. And for the rest of the week, Celeste can't stop thinking of her ex. It's gotten to the point that, almost every night, after the daytime rush of shoots and admin work, she has to touch herself to fall asleep.

Celeste and Gemma barely did anything, just made out, really, but somehow the sheer memory of kissing Gemma again—and how it felt to have her hands on her breasts—is more arousing than anything she's experienced in the last eight years.

Celeste told herself she wasn't going to do anything with Gemma, and yet, the first moment they were alone, she couldn't stop herself from crossing the point of no return. Impulse control had never been one of Celeste's strong points. It's one of the main things that got her into trouble when she was growing up in Seoul, since she'd often kiss other girls—with their full, *breathless* consent, of course—even when she knew she wasn't supposed to.

Most of the time, they managed to keep things a secret, but on the couple occasions they got caught, Celeste's parents would have to move her to another school because the other parents complained, saying that she'd "turned their daughters gay." As if that were a real thing.

Unfortunately, in the highly traditional and homophobic social circles she grew up in, people believed that shit. Which is why, by the time she was a second year in high school, she made it her life goal to go to college in another country, self-studying English as much as she could so she wouldn't be limited to schools close to home.

Sure, it meant she had to study more than her peers, but, in retrospect, everything worked out in Celeste's favor. She learned enough English to get into a college in Los Angeles, where she could freely be herself. And where she met Gemma, for better or for worse.

The night before she's supposed to see Gemma again, Celeste is up late, trying to distract herself from thoughts of her ex. But even that miserably fails when she finishes watching her friends' Instagram Stories and opens Facebook.

These days, the only reason she even still uses the social media app is to scroll through new posts on SASS, an international sapphic Asian group she's in, and Twilight Sewerposting, a meme group with silly, often nonsensical content related to the *Twilight* movies. But today, before she can navigate to any of those pages, the first post that shows up on her feed is a throwback that reads, On this day...

Surrounded by a nostalgic frame is a cute photo collage that Gemma made of their first and only date to Disneyland. Celeste didn't even know she still had this picture, since it never popped up on her Facebook Memories in the last eight years.

Gemma must have unblocked her from social media. The realization makes Celeste's lips twitch with amusement.

In the Disneyland pictures, both she and Gemma are wearing Minnie Mouse ears and posing with various Disney characters. And eating things she doesn't dare consume now because of the probable heartburn, like greasy turkey legs and giant sodas.

Celeste zooms in on the photos and is struck by how young they both look, like they could be friends with the couples they interviewed last week. In her head, college seems like it was just yesterday, but the pictures are jarringly clear evidence that it wasn't.

Flipping through other pictures of herself and Gemma, Celeste finally drifts asleep.

Gemma

When I show up to the studio for our second set of interviews, Celeste gives me a tight-lipped grin. Even with makeup on, she has visible dark circles underneath her eyes. If we were still dating, I'd ask her if she slept okay, but since we're not, I only ask, "Hey, are you ready?"

She, in turn, only replies with "Yeah."

"Okay, great."

I hand her the small paper bag I've put her clothes in. She takes it with a small nod of thanks.

I want to ask Celeste if she's been thinking of me as much as I've been thinking of her, if she still can't get over what happened on Sunday like I can't. But besides our unusually long message exchange on Monday, we barely talked to each other for the rest of the week. And now, she's not even meeting my gaze.

We sit silently in the studio and wait for the couples to arrive.

Today, we're interviewing two millennial married couples. The first one we're supposed to interview—the Amatos—doesn't show up for their time slot, so we decide to move on to the second couple.

Brent Thomas and Aaron Pullman are a white gay couple in their early forties who are "living the blessed child-free, and thus worry-free, life."

"My sister, Bethany, has two kids, and being a guncle for them is fulfilling enough for me," explains Brent. "We also have two cute little Maltipoos that keep us plenty busy."

He shows us pictures of the dogs from his Instagram. They're basically two extremely cute balls of fur, one tan and one white, that are so cute I exclaim, "They're adorable!"

Celeste grins at my outburst and snaps a photo of the moment.

When I ask the couple how they met, Brent answers, "We met at a club here in the city. It was . . . *Jesus*, it's already been fifteen years!"

"Ew," Aaron says jokingly. "You mean I've somehow been with your sorry ass for that long? Was I sober for much of it?"

Brent laughs. "Were you? Because I wasn't."

From behind her cameras, Celeste stifles a laugh.

"We're kidding, obviously," Aaron says with a grin. "But we do go out a lot."

When I tell them about the club I went to with my friends recently, Brent gasps.

"Okay, that one is good, but we usually go to gay clubs,

like Oasis," he says. "I don't do drag anymore, but I still love watching the shows."

We spend a good ten minutes—that we'll have to cut the majority of—talking about the best clubs in San Francisco and about the difficulties of saving for retirement when you live in the city.

"There's so much going on all the time here," Brent says. "Luckily Aaron is good with money, so he takes care of all that for us."

"I work in finance," Aaron explains. "Brent, however..." He sighs.

Brent laughs. "Fine, I admit it," he says. "I'm an influencer, although I do prefer the term 'content creator.' I used to be in tech but...what can I say? My work keeps me young, and I enjoy it. During lockdown, I started documenting our day-to-day lives on social media and people loved it enough for me to make this my full-time job!"

"That's so cool!" I reply. "Congratulations."

"He posts about our dog children a lot," Aaron says. "I think that helps."

"So true. The internet *loves* dogs," Brent agrees. "Even the parts of it that don't like old gay guys like us."

"You're not old," I reply automatically.

Brent raises his eyebrows. "You try turning forty, and then we'll talk. You're what, twenty? Thirty?"

I give him a sheepish smile. "Twenty-nine."

Brent and Aaron scoff.

"So, barely an adult," Aaron says.

"Enjoy that natural collagen while it lasts," quips Brent.

"We're almost forty-five, and I swear to god, my face sags more and more each year."

Eventually, I circle us back to my usual set of questions, wrapping up with what I ask every couple: "What are your plans for the future?"

"Our plans for the future…" Brent trails off. He and Aaron look at each other.

"Well, when were in our thirties, we toyed with the idea of adopting kids," Aaron says. "Or using an egg donor, a surrogate, you know, the whole deal. But we ultimately decided it's not for us. We're far too busy for kids. I'm always working late, and Brent takes trips in other countries for entire months, sometimes. So, we just want to keep being good guncles. And continue to live out our best healthy and happy lives."

Brent nods. "Which sounds cheesy," he adds. "But not really if you factor in the fact that an entire generation of our community elders was affected by the AIDS crisis. Being gay and living long, happy lives is not something we'll ever take for granted."

Aaron solemnly nods in agreement.

"Yeah, that's definitely understandable," I say. "Okay, one last question. How do you define love?"

"Being disgusting together," answers Brent. "Disgustingly cute, disgustingly happy, and disgustingly sad."

Aaron shoots Brent an amused look before turning back to me. "A raison d'être. If it weren't for Brent, my life would just be a lot of numbers, booze, and meaningless sex."

Brent shoots me a knowing glance. "That's how he says

'I love you.'" He gives Aaron a peck on the lips. "I love you, too, babe."

We all laugh, and from behind the cameras, Celeste makes a heart with her fingers.

~

After Aaron and Brent leave, Celeste and I are packing up for the day when I get a call from the Amatos. I put my phone on speaker so Celeste can hear the conversation, too. "Hello?"

"Hi, this is Maria Amato. My husband and I were scheduled to interview with you guys today but couldn't make it because something came up. Sorry, but can we reschedule our interview? Things have been so hectic with our girls out of school for winter break. Weekends work better."

I exchange glances with Celeste, who nods. We reschedule the Amatos for two days later, the Saturday before the week of Christmas. After I hang up, I shoot Evelyn a quick email to inform her about the schedule change.

"Any fun plans for the holiday?" Celeste asks as I get ready to go home.

I turn around to face her. Her expression is neutral, like she's making conversation for the sake of it. Maybe she is. Maybe she's not. It's hard for me to tell what Celeste is thinking these days.

"Not really. I'm going back down to Irvine to spend it with my parents," I reply. "Whenever I'm in town for the holiday, we usually go to Christmas Eve Mass and have family dinner."

Celeste's eyebrows shoot up. "Oh, right, you're Catholic. Do your parents know that you're..."

She trails off. She must be remembering all my anxiety spirals from back when we were in college, when I was still coming to terms with the fact that I'm bi and was so scared that my parents would find out. Back then, my highly traditional parents finding out about my sexuality seemed like a worst nightmare situation, since I'd heard about other kids who were Korean, Christian, or both being disowned for coming out as gay.

"Yeah," I reply. "I was terrified for the longest time, but after I met my friends, Val and Kiara, here in SF...I felt safer and more confident about everything. The first time we all went to Pride together, my parents saw the pictures on social media and had a lot of questions. I was shaking the entire time, but I came out to them. They were surprisingly more ambivalent about it than I thought they'd be. Not totally accepting like the picture-perfect parents on TV, but not opposed to it, either. Although I think they still secretly want me to end up with a man."

Celeste winces. "And you can't even tell them you're not interested in guys. Because you are."

"Right," I sigh. "How about you? If I'm remembering correctly...your parents have known for a while now, right?"

She nods. "Yup. I was a bit of a wild kid, especially by Korean standards. And ever since I first got caught kissing a girl in middle school, they've known I'm not straight. They still wish I was, though," she adds with a bitter laugh. "That's part of the reason why I moved back to LA as soon as my mom was able to take care of herself. Honestly one *great* thing about my parents' divorce is that now I only have one parent who actively pressures me to settle down with a man. I haven't heard from my dad in eight years, and honestly? Good riddance."

"That's so tough," I reply. "I'm sorry."

By then, I've finished packing, and Celeste walks me to the door of the studio.

"It is what it is," she says. "Luckily, I have a chosen family in LA and a close friend in Seoul who gets it. He's coming to hang out with us for Christmas this year, staying with me for a week before traveling elsewhere in the country."

"Oh, that sounds so fun!" I exclaim. "Is this the friend that helped you while you were having a hard time back home?"

Celeste nods. "Yup. His name is Min-joon. We've been friends since we were kids. That's actually one of the reasons I know I'm definitely lesbian," she adds in a dry, vaguely humorous tone. "Because if I liked men, we'd be married by now."

A giggle escapes from my lips. "Wait, and he doesn't like you in that way, either?"

She shrugs. "Well, unlike Aaron and Brent, he's bi, not gay. So I guess there's always that possibility. But no, apparently I'm too scary to be his type. He claims he can barely tolerate me as a friend."

This time, I can't stop myself from full-on hollering. "Too scary!"

Celeste shrugs again, but she's smiling now, too.

It's raining outside, so after Celeste and I wish each other a happy holiday, I stay inside the lobby to request a car to my friends' place. I do have my umbrella, so theoretically, I *could* walk to the bus, ride it to the light rail stop, and take the train to Inner Sunset. But I don't want to deal with the cold rain, and especially not at night.

As I wait for my ride, I realize this was the first time in a while that Celeste and I had an extensive, personal conversation together. It was nice, but also strangely foreign, like putting on a favorite cardigan that had been lost under the bed for several years.

My car arrives, and as I get in, I wonder if Celeste and I could possibly be friends again, chatting for hours like we did before we even officially dated. Celeste talking about her friend Min-joon made me slightly jealous, not because of anything romantic, but because I wished I also had that kind of friendship with someone. I love Kiara and Val, but it'd be nice to have a friend who's queer *and* shares the same cultural background as me.

I stare down at my phone, wondering if I should ask Celeste to just be friends. But then, I get a flash of us on Sunday, of how I was seconds away from ripping off her clothes. With a sigh, I rest my head on the window and close my eyes, listening to the *pitter-patter* of the rain.

Gemma

The next day at work, Evelyn sticks her head out of her office door as I walk by.

"Gemma?" she says. "A word, please."

I sent her the materials for Brent and Aaron's interview last night, so when I enter the room, I ask, "Was there an issue with the third interview?"

Evelyn blinks. "What? No, it was fantastic. You did a fabulous job getting the couple to open up. There's something else related to the project that I wanted to talk to you about."

I brace myself, wondering what it could be, but even then, I'm wholly unprepared when Evelyn says, "You and Celeste should come to the New Year's Eve party."

At first, I think I misheard her. My boss, telling me to come to an office party…with my ex? Did I somehow hit my head and fall into one of my worst nightmares?

"Several representatives from Citrine will be present, and it will be a nice chance for you two to network and sell them on the cover story, since we'll be finalizing that decision in a few weeks."

I freeze. For as long as I've been at *Horizon*, the office NYE party has always been James's and my thing, since we went together for the last seven years. I'd been too busy dealing with my clusterfuck of a personal life to even *think* about this year's, but now, I panic. New Year's Eve is in less than two weeks. James is probably going to be there with Daphne. And Evelyn specifically wants me to go to the party with *Celeste*.

"Of course, I can't force you to do anything," Evelyn continues when I don't respond. "But take some time to think about it. It's a great opportunity!"

"I'm not sure if it'd be a good idea for us to come to the party," I say at last. "But I'll ask Celeste."

I'm still thinking about the sheer ridiculous notion of inviting my college ex to the end-of-year party when I enter the studio on Saturday morning. I'm late, so I expect to see the Amatos waiting for me with Celeste. But only Celeste is there, typing away at a large Mac desktop in the corner of the studio. I didn't even realize there was a computer in this space until now.

"This part's usually sectioned off," Celeste says when she sees my confused expression. As I watch, she pulls on the tall curtains at the edge of the room. Sure enough, when they're spread out again, I see the studio space I'd grown accustomed to in the last couple of weeks.

"The Amatos called," she goes on. "They're running late because their babysitter canceled on them last minute. I told them they could bring the kids. Hope that's okay."

I balk, looking around at all the expensive equipment in the rented studio. "Are you sure?"

She nods. "Yup, I'm good with kids. They can play on the couch while we interview their parents."

I notice only then that she's moved the couch behind the cameras, replacing it with two chairs from the dining table.

As we wait for the Amatos to arrive, I remember a conversation we had back in college, when Celeste told me she's the oldest cousin on both sides of her family.

"All my aunts and uncles used me as a babysitter," she'd said with a laugh. "And I never minded, since I loved kids. Still do, actually."

Thirty minutes later, Maria and Joey Amato arrive with their two daughters, Carly and Kaylee, in tow. Both Carly and Kaylee can't be more than seven. Carly, with her blond curls and hazel eyes, resembles Joey, while Kaylee resembles Maria with her tan skin, dark brown hair, and almost black eyes. Within minutes, the girls are running around the studio, shrieking with joy when they see the huge windows and fancy equipment.

Maria shoots us an apologetic look. Joey glances back at the door, as if already reconsidering their decision to come to the studio.

"I got this," Celeste says, setting her camera down on the kitchen table.

I watch as she kneels down and stretches her arms out toward the screaming children in a "come here" gesture.

"Hey, girls," she says in a soft, gentle tone I've never heard her use before. "Why don't you come here for a sec?"

Surely that won't work... I don't even finish my thought before Carly and Kaylee run to her and take her hands.

"How are you two doing?" Celeste says, gently swaying both their arms back and forth.

"Good!" declares Carly.

"I'm okay," says Kaylee.

"Well, that's good to hear," Celeste says to Carly. With a smile, she then tells Kaylee, "And I hope your day gets better, sweetheart. We're going to have some fun today, okay? My name is Celeste. And my friend, Gemma, and I are going to interview your mommy and daddy for a few minutes."

Carly claps her hands in excitement. "An interview! How cool!"

"Right? Well, you'll be able to watch the video with them after it's done, on Valentine's Day! Won't that be neat? But before you can do that, we need your help. All right, girls?"

Kaylee shyly nods and smiles up at Celeste, absolutely smitten. And I don't blame her. Celeste is always charismatic, but like this, she's mesmerizing. At this moment, we're all caught under her spell.

An alternative timeline flashes in my head, one where

Celeste didn't disappear and she and I stayed together for the last eight years. We'd probably have kids by now, either through adoption or other means. Back when we were in college, Celeste would always talk about how much she wanted kids of her own someday. And even though I myself have always been more ambivalent about them, I was still looking forward to getting to that point with Celeste one day, back when I thought we had a future together.

"I have to get your parents ready for the big interview," I hear Celeste say to the kids. "But meanwhile, why don't you two play some fun games on my tablet with Gemma over there?"

I freeze as everyone suddenly turns to me. The last time I played with kids was in college, when I volunteered at a local elementary school. Luckily, I got assigned the older grades, so none of the kids I supervised were as young as Kaylee and Carly. But I still take the tablet from Celeste and make a "come here" gesture in an attempt to emulate my ex.

"Video games!" Kaylee yells, no longer shy.

The girls jump up and down with joy.

Luckily, both Kaylee and Carly become quickly obsessed with *Crossy Road*, and they don't even look up from the screen when Celeste says, "Okay, we're all set and ready to go."

I leave the kids on the couch and settle into my usual chair by Celeste's cameras. I ask the Amatos my usual list of questions, starting off with how they met.

"We met in college," Maria says.

"We were in the same co-ed dorm freshman year and couldn't keep our hands off each other," Joey adds.

Maria blushes and I give them a polite smile. "That's amazing. And how long have you two been together?"

"Over a decade now," Maria replies.

"Time goes by so fast, doesn't it?" Joey shares a smile with his wife. "Who knew back then that we'd be actual adults now, all settled into our new house with our two kids? There were lots of times we thought we couldn't do it, what with the economy and all. But thankfully we pulled through, in the end."

"Yup. It all worked out. And all because we have each other," Maria adds. "Which sounds cheesy, I know. But it's true. Joey has been my rock through it all."

"And she's been *my* rock," Joey says with a grin. "It's funny, though, because we went from being complete kids who just had huge crushes on each other to... this." He waves his hand at the two of them, and then at the girls on the couch. "If you asked me what love was back then, I'd have a completely different perception of what it is, compared to the one I have now."

Maria laughs. "Right? In college, I thought love was about flowers and chocolates. Or cute dates or trips around the world. But what it actually is most days is, 'Hey, I can play with the kids so you can go nap.'"

We all laugh.

"We do still like to spoil each other with fancy things once in a while," Joey says. "But most days, a nap is the best present in the world."

"What were some of the biggest challenges in your relationship?" I ask, moving on to the next question.

"All the surprises," answers Joey. "And the random road bumps we hit along the way."

"The surprises!" Maria exclaims. "Yes, oh my gosh, Joe, remember when we first found out I was pregnant with Carly? We thought our worlds were ending."

Joey laughs. "Oh, wow, yeah, I think I blocked it out or something, because I'm only remembering it now."

"I was applying for law school when I got pregnant with our first," Maria explains. "And Joey had just started his job. We were already married by then, thankfully, but we thought we'd have more time by ourselves."

Joey glances over at where the girls are playing on the couch.

"Protection doesn't always work," he whispers to one of Celeste's video cameras.

Celeste, who'd been about to snap a picture, stops to raise her eyebrows at him.

"Sorry," Joey adds before continuing in a normal volume, "we became parents earlier than we thought we would, but if I could go back in time, I wouldn't change a thing."

"Definitely not," agrees Maria. "Although, sometimes I do wonder what my life would be like if I *had* gone to law school and become a big-shot lawyer like I wanted to."

I frown. "Do you regret not going to law school?"

She laughs. "Oh, no. In my twenties, the idea of being a lawyer in a fast-paced work environment seemed like the dream, but in retrospect, I'm glad I didn't go down that path. I work part-time in another field now, and sure it's less pay, but it's great since I get so much more flexibility *and* time to spend with the girls. Or with Joey or by myself," she adds with a laugh. "I'm so content with my life now."

"And we're lucky to have her," Joey says. "We all are."

They share a sweet forehead kiss, which Celeste rapidly snaps a photo of. The moment is picture-perfect, and I have no doubt it will look even more precious on camera.

Before I can stop it, an ugly pang of jealousy hits my stomach. A long-term relationship that actually became a marriage. A home and a family to call my own. Sure, it's all a bit traditional. But I *wanted* that life. It was my dream, one that I wanted so much that I was willing to change who I was. And that, I now realize, was the problem. I'm angry at James for changing his mind, but I'm also angry at myself for being so stupid. For thinking everything would be fine if I just went with the flow.

Some of my college friends already have kids like Carly and Kaylee. Meanwhile, I don't even have a place to call my own right now, and in a cruel twist of fate, I'm working with *my college ex* of all people. I'm only going backward, pushed away from the shore by an insurmountable wave.

I feel a little lightheaded, but I press on.

"What are some of your future plans?" It takes all my effort to keep my voice steady, but I manage. Or at least, I think I do. But then Maria and Joey give me looks of concern.

"Are you feeling all right?" Maria asks.

"Yeah," I reply. "I mean, I think so..."

I must not have been convincing, because Celeste walks over to the video cameras and pauses the recording. "Why don't we all take a fifteen-minute break?" she says diplomatically. "So the girls can get a break from screen time and everyone who needs it can go to the restroom."

As if on cue, Kaylee says, "Mommy, can I go to the bathroom?"

The couple laughs, and Celeste directs the Amatos to the restroom upstairs. I watch them, but I can't get a sound out myself. The room is spinning, and I can barely breathe.

"Sorry," I finally manage to say. But even then, I'm not sure if anyone can hear me. "I'm gonna get some fresh air."

I rush out of the building as tears start falling from my eyes. The streets are crowded with people heading out for dinner and drinks.

The door slams shut behind me, and some passersby startle at the noise. I ignore them and sit on the ground with my back against the door.

Pulling my legs into my chest, I try to become as small and inconspicuous as possible as I listen to myself breathe. At first, my breaths come in heaves, quick but heavy, before gradually becoming slow and deep.

I'd been doing relatively well in the last couple of weeks, so I thought I was better now. I thought I was over what happened between James and me. But clearly, I'm not. And I'm so sick of not being okay.

The door opens, and I almost fall back. Before I can, firm but gentle hands grip my shoulders and hold me steady.

"Hey," says Celeste.

When I don't say anything in response, Celeste continues, "Do you want me to ask the Amatos if they can come back another time to finish the interview?"

I blink up at her. Her face is blurry because of the tears clouding my vision.

Celeste's eyes widen with concern. "Gem, what's wrong?" Before either of us can think twice, she sits down on the ground and wraps her arms around me. In this one moment, I'm too broken up inside to care how weird it is that, of all people, my college ex is here, comforting me while I try to deal with the pain from my most recent breakup.

"It's…all too much," I quietly say. "Today. Seeing the Amatos. Remembering what I had less than two months ago. I had a *future. A path.*" I know I'm rambling, saying stuff that Celeste doesn't have enough context to understand. But the pain in my chest is too much, exploding out of me like bursts of lava. Celeste, to her credit, is silent, quietly listening as I talk. "I knew who I was and where I was headed. And then, suddenly, boom, nothing. Back to square one. Nothing but a nebulous nothing ahead, all because, after seven years of being together, my ex-fiancé randomly decided he didn't love me anymore and got with someone else, a mere *two weeks* after we broke up."

Celeste frowns. "Wait, hold on. He already moved on?"

I nod. Tears stream down my face again, and I wipe them away as I continue, "What the Amatos have…that's the kind of life I thought was within my grasp. But he replaced me so easily. After *seven years.*"

Celeste lets out a frustrated groan as she leans back against the wall.

"He sounds awfully like my dad," she says. "Except my dad decided he didn't want to be married to my mom after more than twenty years."

I stare wide-eyed at Celeste. She remains completely still as she continues, "Yup, that's how they divorced. *After* my mom got sick, too. I'm telling you, it was a shit show back home. That's part of the reason why I don't do relationships anymore, and why I got so distant with you. What's the point of love if someone can still abandon you after *twenty years*?"

I'm taken aback. As a hopeless romantic, I profoundly and deeply disagree with Celeste's sentiment. But also, it's not like I have the track record to prove myself right.

"I'm so sorry" is all I can say in the end. "That must have been difficult for you and your mom."

Celeste bites her lip and avoids my gaze, staring out into the busy street, instead. I don't have to be an expert in body language to know that this conversation is making her uncomfortable.

"Anyway," she says a few seconds later. "Enough about me. Is it okay if I give you some encouraging words? Would that help you right now? Or would it be too weird considering our history?"

I shrug. "Not at all. Since I have to give people advice as part of my job—where to eat, what to try out, how to deal with relationship problems, et cetera—I love *receiving* advice. It's a nice change."

Celeste gets back on her feet. "Okay, well, there's this quote I always say to myself whenever shit happens, and I'm not even that religious. 'Man makes plans, and God laughs.' We have no idea what's going to happen in life, and even when we think we have it all figured out, everything can come crashing down, anyway. The best we can do is roll with the punches and stop blaming ourselves whenever something goes wrong. Your ex leaving you like that is not your fault at all, *especially* if he's already fucking someone else, just like it's not my mom's fault that my dad now has a girlfriend who's younger than me. Both dudes have serious issues. You're better off, like my mom's better off without my dad."

Celeste's words aren't exactly *encouraging* like she said they'd be, but they do help me feel a bit less alone. "Is your mom doing better now?" I ask. "Not just health-wise, but... everything else."

She nods. "She's been enjoying her single, empty nester life for a while now. Like I said, better off."

"Okay, good." I get back on my feet, too. "Well, thanks for the advice. And for coming down here to get me. Let's go finish the interview. I'd rather complete it now, since we already had to reschedule them once. Are they still up there?"

"Yup. Joey and Maria have their hands full. I think you distracted the girls from the game enough that they want to do something else."

"Great," I say with a bone-weary laugh. Suddenly, I'm afraid I've ruined everything. "How are we going to keep them distracted now?"

"It's no big deal." Celeste says, holding the door open for me. "We can have them play another game. It's okay, Gem. We'll figure it out."

"Why do you keep calling me that?" It's something I've been wondering for a while, but didn't have the chance to ask her until now.

Celeste blinks. "What do you mean?"

"Gem."

She shrugs. "It's a habit, I guess. I can't even remember the last time I called you Gemma. Does it bother you? Because I can say Gemma, if you want."

I take the couple minutes' walk up the stairs to ponder on Celeste's question. When we reach the studio, I say, "It did, at first. But if it's just out of habit, I'm fine with it. Actually, I think it'd be weird if you randomly started calling me Gemma."

Her lips spread into a small smile. "Okay, then. Gem it is."

20

Gemma

Thankfully, Celeste manages to distract the girls with *Plants vs. Zombies*, and I power through the rest of the questions by keeping my own emotions at bay. We finish the interview without any other incident.

Before the family leaves, Celeste asks the couple if they'd like her to take a picture of them.

"We don't have to share it publicly if you don't want us to, but I would love to take a picture of your beautiful family and give it to you as a keepsake," she says. "Consider it a token of appreciation and gratitude for coming out here when you probably have a million things going on right now."

"That's incredibly kind of you," Maria says with a smile. "That would be lovely. Thank you so much!"

The girls crawl into their parents' laps, and the resulting portrait is so adorable that I for sure want to include it in the interview spread for the magazine if the Amatos are okay with it.

When I ask, the couple nods at each other.

"Feel free," Joey says. "I think the family picture would be a nice thing to have on there. After all, love isn't just romantic."

I'm taken aback by Joey's words and how right they are. I think of my parents, who have always loved me and are constantly worrying about me in their little home in Irvine. I think about Val and Kiara, who immediately offered up their place when I needed somewhere to stay and never pressured me to pay rent or contribute in any way.

I may have hilariously tragic luck when it comes to romance, but for other kinds of love, I hit the jackpot.

On their way out, I apologize to the Amatos for earlier, telling them I'm going through a lot in terms of my personal life.

"It happens," Maria graciously says. "I hope things get better for you soon."

"Thank you."

Soon enough, it's just Celeste and me in the studio again. I'm entirely spent, emotionally and physically. It's been one of those days that feels like a whole month. Celeste must have also been exhausted, because she doesn't say anything as we get ready to go home.

"I'll see you for the next interview," I say before I leave. "Safe travels next week."

"See you," she replies. "You, too."

Like all holidays, Christmas comes and goes way too fast. Aside from doing typical holiday things with my parents, I manage to finally find a promising listing for a shared apartment in Chinatown, only a ten-minute bus ride from our office.

When I'm back in town the next Monday, I work out the contract terms with my new landlady, Ms. Chang, who runs a Chinese gift shop with her husband. Since I don't want to commit to anything long term after the last couple of wildcard months I had, I end up signing a month-to-month lease. Luckily, Ms. Chang is flexible, since she's just renting out her spare room to make some extra money after her kid moved out to start school as a spring admit at USC.

We set my move-in date for January 15, which will be perfect timing since that'll be after the holidays *and* after Celeste and I—hopefully—finish all the work we need to do for the project.

Looking forward to the New Year already, I walk into our office, in time to hear one of my coworkers exclaim, "Apparently there's going to be a chocolate fountain this year! I'm *so* excited."

"They could lock us up in a bare concrete room for all I care," replies another. "As long as the bartender is as good as the one from last year."

The company party. With how busy things have been,

I didn't even get a chance to ask Celeste if she wants to go with me. Since it's now the thirtieth, it's probably too short notice. Besides, the last thing I want to do is ring in the New Year while watching James and Daphne work the room together. Maybe it's best if we don't go.

Luckily, as far as company events go, our New Year's party is the most optional, since a lot of people are usually out of town during this time of year. Kiara and Val aren't going, either, since they're on a spontaneous trip to Seattle this week and won't be back until after New Year's Eve.

Evelyn will be disappointed if I choose not to go, especially since Celeste and I will miss out on the networking opportunity. But there's also a good chance that I'm overthinking, and she won't even say anything about it afterward. Or at least I hope she won't.

I'm pretty set on not going when, later that day, James stops by my desk.

"Hey," he says.

It takes me a few seconds to even process he's actually there, talking to me face-to-face after over a month of pretending I don't exist.

Maybe he just needs to talk to me about a work-related thing.

"Yes?" I ask.

"Just making sure, you're not coming to the party tomorrow, right?"

I immediately bristle. "Why?"

"I'm bringing Daphne. And it'd be awkward if you were there, too, since we used to go to the party together."

I can hardly believe my ears. Granted, I'd wanted to avoid the awkwardness, too. But the way James has the nerve to tell me what to do, after everything he's done to me... When we were still dating, whenever James asked me to do something, I either told him yes or said "I'll think about it" when I actually meant "no." Today, though, I snap.

"Let me get this straight. You want me to not go to the office party, the one that's open to *all* employees, so things won't be awkward for you and your new girlfriend?"

James blinks and shrugs like a malfunctioning robot, obviously taken aback. "Yeah? I don't get why that's a big deal. You hate parties, anyway."

I hate parties? Anger washes over me like a giant wave, crashing and raging inside my chest. My first instinct is to tell James off and yell at him to go away.

But then, I get a better idea.

"For your information," I say. "I love parties. I stopped going to them because of *you*. And I'm already planning on attending tomorrow. With a date."

James's eyes narrow with skepticism. "A date?"

I lift up my chin. "Yup."

It's so last minute, I doubt Celeste will agree to go. I'm not even completely sure if she's back from LA yet, since we haven't said a word to each other after the day we interviewed the Amatos. But James doesn't need to know that.

"Well, okay," he says, taking a step back with a huff. "Guess it can't be helped, then."

For the first time since we broke up, he looks *pissed*. Which both surprises and amuses me to no end. Celeste will probably say no, but at this point, I don't care. Because the deep satisfaction I get at James's expression is plenty enough revenge.

21 Celeste

The last thing Celeste expects on the second-to-last day of the year is a phone call from Gemma. Lately, she and her ex have only ever communicated through email or KakaoTalk. Although they converse in person just fine—or as well as they can, given the circumstances—the sheer concept of talking with her ex on the phone is so daunting she lets it ring all the way to voicemail before calling her back.

She doesn't know what to expect when Gemma picks up, but her ex's retelling of all the drama surrounding a *company party* holds her captivated. Celeste enjoys being her own boss, but the one thing she misses about working at an office is all the drama and politics. She loves being able to hear about everything without being directly involved.

Celeste can't remember the last time she and Gemma talked on the phone like this, but it surprisingly feels...

normal. It of course isn't as natural as talking to her actual friends, but it's not as bad as she thought it would be.

"Let me get this straight," Celeste says when Gemma finishes her story. "Your ex-fiancé told you to not come to the party so he can go to it with his new girlfriend? What an asshole. Men really are the worst."

"Yeah..." Gemma replies. "And I know it wasn't my place to say this, but the only way I could think of telling him off was by saying I'm attending with a date."

Celeste lets her ex's words sink in for a beat. And then another. "And I'm assuming that's where I come in?"

"Yup. Again, no worries at all if you don't want to. I just said it to piss him off—"

"I'll come," Celeste cuts in. There's something very tantalizing about the chance to see for herself the man who *dared* to replace her in Gemma's life. The work aspect is another huge perk, which Gemma had mentioned in her account. "It'll be good for the project if we went together, right? Why don't we kill two birds with one stone? Piss off your ex-fiancé *and* secure our chances of a cover story. I want this cover, Gem. It'll be my very first one."

Gemma groans. "Your Gemini and Capricorn placements are showing."

Celeste is taken aback by the random segue. When her brain catches up, she asks, "You remember my signs?"

Gemma sighs dramatically. "Gemini Sun, Capricorn Moon, and Scorpio Rising. But also, Gemini Venus and Virgo Mars. Basically, a hot workaholic who loves drama but hates emotions."

A surprised laugh escapes from Celeste's mouth. "Gem," she says. "And what are you . . . a Pisces?"

Astrology is a common gay pastime, and many of Celeste's queer friends—especially the ones who live in LA—are deeply involved in it, sometimes even using things like astrocartography to determine where to travel or relocate. Meanwhile, she herself always has trouble remembering the different signs and who is what.

"Yup," Gemma says with another loud sigh. "Pisces Sun, Taurus Moon, and Cancer Rising. With a Leo Mars and Aquarius Venus at that. Basically, a stubborn ball of water that loves people a bit too much."

"I don't know that much about astrology, but I know enough to know that I love your Big Three. I have friends with some of the exact same placements. So adorable."

"Even if it makes me a stubborn ball of emotions?"

"A *cute* ball of emotions." The moment she says it, Celeste bites her lip. Somehow, they've gotten dangerously close to flirting.

Gemma clears her throat. "Anyway, I have to go. I'll text you the information about the party. Thanks for agreeing to do this last minute. And for listening to me vent."

"Great," Celeste says. She does her best to switch gears so her tone is once again clipped and professional. "And you're welcome. See you."

She hangs up, hoping she didn't make a huge mistake.

22

Gemma

The dress code for the office NYE party is always ugly Christmas sweaters. It's a tradition that goes back several years to one fateful day when someone in the office—Shane, probably—lamented that he never got to see anyone's ugly Christmas sweaters because people were always gone for the holiday. It's a quirky idea that stuck, mostly because everyone was glad to have another excuse to wear their ugly Christmas sweaters before packing them up for another year.

In the past, James and I got matching ones, wearing anything from slightly inappropriate designs like snowmen that had carrot stick dicks and boobs, to cute and wholesome ones like Santa and Mrs. Claus. I have no idea if Celeste will want to wear matching Christmas sweaters, since we never wore coupley outfits when we dated in college. But I buy a pair for us anyway. I can always return them if she says no.

Because it's so last minute—and almost a week past Christmas—the sweaters I find at a nearby thrift store are basic but still, I think, pretty cute. Both are bright Christmas red with white text on them. One says SANTA while the other one simply says BABY. And the best part is, they're professional enough to wear while talking to the higher-ups without explicitly denoting any sort of relationship label whatsoever.

I send Celeste a picture of the sweaters a few hours before the party.

Adorable, she replies, along with a laughing emoji.

Who should wear "Santa" and who should wear "Baby?"

Celeste replies almost instantly with Well, you're obviously "Baby."

Back in college, Celeste usually called me Gem. But on rare occasions, she called me "Gemma baby," especially when she was feeling particularly romantic or when we were in bed together.

My heart speeds up. I don't know how or when it happened, but at some point down the line, Celeste and I stopped being strictly professional with each other. It makes my stomach flutter nervously, but if I'm being honest with myself, I kind of like it. It's nice to not have to be so stiff and formal around Celeste anymore. Regardless of whatever's going on between us.

Since no one else—including Burrito—is at the apartment tonight, I invite Celeste over so she can change into her sweater before we head out for the party. When I answer the door with my BABY sweater on, her face softens.

"Very cute," she says.

That is definitely *not* the response I have when *she* comes out of the bathroom in her sweater. With her black leather skirt, tied-back hair, and knee-high white leather boots, she gives her "Santa" sweater an edge that screams more "Daddy" than "St. Nick."

I never thought I could find someone in a Christmas sweater so *hot* before, but I stand corrected.

"Thanks again for doing this," I tell Celeste on our way to the venue. "And sorry in advance for any awkwardness that might ensue at this party. Hopefully it'll be somewhat entertaining, though. And we'll have a productive conversation with the higher-ups."

"No worries at all," she replies. "Honestly, I'm excited. I've never been to an office holiday party before. One of the downsides of not working a traditional nine-to-five."

She has an uncharacteristically giddy grin on her face. It's cute, but also a little disorienting.

"A downside?" I ask. "Trust me, you're not missing much."

"Oh?"

"Most people only go to this one because of the open bar. And the fact that it's free for employees, while most NYE parties in the city are expensive. Even then, a lot of people like my friends still opt to go somewhere else that's *not* related to work. They're in Seattle right now with their cat."

As we approach the venue, I feel lightheaded. Bringing Celeste seemed like a good idea when I first thought of it, but now that we're mere steps away from pitching directly to the Citrine execs—something I've never even done by myself—and her meeting my coworkers, I'm less sure.

I take a few slow breaths and turn to Celeste, who gives me a concerned look.

"You okay?" she asks.

"Yeah. Or at least I think I am."

"Don't sweat too much about this, okay? Sure, it'd be nice, but if we don't get the cover, it's not the end of the world. And fuck your ex, really."

I raise my eyebrows. "Do you know how ironic it is for you to tell me that last part?"

She lets out a sharp laugh. "Yeah, I heard it the moment I said it."

"But yeah, okay. Let's try to have as much fun as we can after we meet with the higher-ups, then. There's apparently going to be a chocolate fountain, in addition to the open bar."

Celeste rubs her hands together in anticipation. "My kind of party."

When we enter through the doors, everyone turns to stare at us. It's only then that I realize I never explicitly told anyone at work besides Evelyn, James, and my friends that I like women, too.

Oops.

Luckily, since we're in San Francisco, most people just give me a look of mild surprise before going back to what they were doing. That is, everyone except James.

James's mouth drops open when he sees me and Celeste. Shock, confusion, and anger flash across his face in rapid succession before his mouth closes again, becoming a straight, displeased line. It's the most I've seen him emote since our breakup.

"Look behind me," I whisper to Celeste. "At the white guy with brown hair and blue eyes. The one that's staring at us. That's him. My ex-fiancé."

"Ah," Celeste says in a low voice. "Noted. Also, Gem, try to relax a bit. You're visibly tense."

I shake my arms and legs to loosen myself up a bit. "Better?"

"Much better."

"Okay, let's look for Evelyn. She's probably with the—"

"Gemma!" The loud clip-clops of high heels echo throughout the room as Evelyn glides toward us in her long chiffon dress like a debutante at a ball. Every year, Evelyn is the only person at the party decidedly *not* wearing a Christmas sweater.

"Perfect timing. We were *just* talking about your project. And Celeste! I'm happy you could also make it."

Celeste extends her hand in Evelyn's direction, putting on her charm at full force. "It's so nice to see you, too! Thank you again for having me on this project. I'm enjoying it so far."

Evelyn shakes Celeste's hand after giving me a curious

glance. "The pleasure is all mine. Gemma's been sending me your amazing work for this project. Let me introduce you two to some of the representatives of Citrine, our parent company."

Evelyn leads us to a small circle of four people of various ages and ethnicities. I let Celeste do most of the talking, since it's her photography that's going to be on the cover. I'm pleased—but not surprised—to see Celeste has prepared examples, from both the interviews and her previous shoots, to show everyone on her phone. As I watch her pitch herself, I can't help but feel an immense sense of pride. I suddenly wish we were dating again, so I can kiss her and tell her how amazing she is.

"Oh, this is so lovely," says one woman as she looks at Celeste's work. I don't know her by name, but I recognize her face from a picture I saw of our board of directors. "You have a wonderful way of capturing people in your photos."

"Thank you," Celeste says. "It's also thanks to Gemma, who is a great interviewer. She helps people open up and get comfortable so they don't look nervous on camera."

Everyone turns to me. Luckily, I prepared my own pitch. After properly introducing myself, I jump into it and wrap up by saying, "Everyone loves love, whether they'd like to admit it to themselves or not. And since we're all a bit nosy, we get curious about other people and how they live their lives. So, I strongly believe this topic of modern love, as well as Celeste's beautiful cover, will catch people's attention and appeal to a broad demographic of people in the city and beyond."

The representatives look impressed with our pitch, and afterward, as Evelyn leads us away, she says, "Excellent job, you two. Now, please do enjoy the rest of the party. And do check out the chocolate fountain when you have the chance. Happy New Year!"

She winks and gives my shoulder an encouraging squeeze before gliding away.

After a brief detour at the chocolate fountain—which is worth *all* the hype—we grab some drinks from the bar and head to the dance floor. But before we're able to fully enjoy ourselves, we come face-to-face with James and Daphne.

James's face is stony and deceptively calm, so I wouldn't think he was upset if I didn't know him well. But since I do, I know this is his *immense rage* face, which I'd thankfully only seen a few times in the last seven years.

Daphne stays a few steps behind him, looking between the three of us with raised eyebrows.

"Gemma," James says, bringing my attention back to him. "Happy New Year."

"Hi, James," I reply. "Happy New Year to you, too. Celeste, this is James. James, this is Celeste."

Daphne doesn't make any move to introduce herself, and honestly, I can't blame her. I wouldn't say anything, either, if I were in her super-awkward position.

At the sound of Celeste's name, James winces, like he was hoping it wasn't her and I confirmed his worst nightmare. While he and I dated, we did talk about each other's exes, so her name must have rung a bell. He turns his body toward me like he's trying to exclude Celeste from the conversation. "Is she...a friend?" he asks.

There's a twinge of desperation in his eyes, like he *wishes* Celeste and I were just friends.

I can't believe he has the gall to hope that Celeste and I are "just friends," even after I told him I was bringing a date. Since we're surrounded by our coworkers, I try to figure out how to tell him "fuck off" in a civil way. But before I can, Celeste wraps an arm around my waist.

"We're together," she says. "So, much more than friends."

Gemma

Together?

Even though I know Celeste is putting up a front for my sake, hearing her say those words *in front of James* sends a thrill down my spine.

James coughs and shifts in obvious discomfort.

"Well, good luck, then," he says. He has the nerve to look a bit hurt. *How do you like the taste of your own medicine?*

I stare him down until he finally breaks eye contact to turn back to Daphne. "Come on, let's say hi to more people."

Celeste's lips slide into a mischievous grin as they leave.

When they're out of earshot, she lets go of me and asks, "Well? How'd I do? Not bad right?"

I laugh. "You're loving this."

"I am," she admits. "He's *such* a prick."

And then finally, *finally*, we're enjoying ourselves, having so much fun drinking and dancing that I lose track of time. Even so, I'm shocked when the DJ stops the music to announce, "All right, folks, we're approaching the last fifteen minutes of the year. Grab a flute of champagne and your special someone before it's too late!"

"It's almost midnight already?" My words come out slurred, and I'm barely standing up straight on my own two feet. I *may* have drunk a bit too much, but so has almost everyone else in the room. "Wow, that bartender mixes some very strong drinks."

"He does," Celeste agrees, picking up two champagne flutes from one of the waiters. "But also, you're a lightweight. I think you only had two or three?"

"Do you not feel it?"

"Kinda. I could drink a lot more, but *one* of us has to make sure we get home safely."

Even though I'm pretty far gone, I'm sober enough to feel bad that Celeste has to be the responsible one at *my* office party.

"Noooo," I say. "Have fun! We're not even driving afterward."

"It's fine. Besides, who says I'm not having fun? Watching you trying to dance in this state is the best entertainment I've had all week."

As if on cue, I lose my balance, nearly toppling onto the floor.

"Whoa there!" Celeste catches me just in time, pulling me back on my feet so we're almost nose to nose.

I want to kiss her. So bad. I close my eyes, too drunk to care about anything else.

But instead of making out with me like I want her to, Celeste coughs. "Gem, your boss is watching."

"Huh?"

I straighten up, my vision blurring from the sudden movement. As soon as I'm able, I search the dance floor. No Evelyn in sight.

"I'm kidding," Celeste laughs. "I have no idea where she is."

I laugh, too, but my heart squeezes with disappointment. I was clearly about to kiss her when she pulled that little trick. It makes me wonder if she hasn't been feeling the same tension I've been feeling between us all night.

We are *exes, after all*... I remind myself. But I'd be lying if I said I still hold the same resentment and bitterness I felt toward her when we first ran into each other last month.

"Okay!" the DJ exclaims. "The time has come! Lift your champagne flutes and get ready to ring in the New Year! Ten...nine..."

Celeste gently but firmly hoists me up so I'm standing straight again.

"Eight...seven..."

I look up at Celeste, and she peers down at me, the faintest smile on her face as she hands me my champagne flute.

"Six...five...four..."

We squeeze each other's hands.

"Three...two...one...HAPPY NEW YEAR!"

Confetti explodes all around us as people raise their champagne flutes high in the air.

"Happy New Year, Gemma baby," says Celeste.

She kisses my forehead, and fireworks explode inside my chest.

~

We're getting into our Uber when I realize that I left my keys on the kitchen counter of my friends' apartment. I'd been so distracted and nervous about the night ahead that I left for the party without them. Luckily, the front door locks automatically, so I don't have to worry about a New Year's home invasion. But unfortunately, that also means I'm very much locked out, and my friends aren't coming back until this afternoon.

"Shit," I say, leaning my head back against the car seat. My mouth is parched, and my head's pounding already. I forgot to drink water the entire night. I'm trying to figure out what to do, when Celeste says, "Let's go back to my place. It's closer, anyway."

She changes our destination on her phone before I can protest.

Fortunately—or unfortunately, depending on how you look at it—I'm sobered up by the time we reach Celeste's apartment. Unlike the last time I ended up here, I'm not blissfully asleep, so when the front door clicks closed behind us, leaving Celeste and me alone in the darkness of her apartment, I awkwardly stare at her, unsure what to do.

After we take off our shoes, Celeste stares back at me for a moment before flicking on the lights and making herself busy by bringing me a towel, toiletries, and everything else

I'd need for the night. She even gets me a pair of silky soft pink pajamas.

"So you don't have to sleep in a scratchy Christmas sweater," she says with a slight smile.

"Thanks," I reply, genuinely grateful for her hospitality. It's not the kind of treatment I'd ever expect from an ex. "Sorry, can I also have a glass of water?" I ask. "I'm so dehydrated right now. I accidentally forgot to drink some all night."

Celeste groans. "Suddenly, we're back in college again," she says as she pours me a glass. "Remember how I had to always remind you to drink water whenever we went out? Sorry I didn't do that this time around. I was too focused on everything that was going on tonight."

I wince. "It's not your fault. Or your responsibility. I led you into a lion's den."

"It was fun, though," she says. "Really. Quite a memorable way to start the New Year."

Our fingers touch as she hands me the glass. It's the briefest moment of physical contact, but it still makes me shudder with pleasure. Hoping the water will cool me down in more ways than one, I gulp down the entire glass. But when I finish, I catch sight of Celeste staring down at my now wet lips.

I bite my bottom lip, and she briefly closes her eyes.

"Gem," she says, her voice low and breathless. "What are we doing?" She sounds almost pained.

"I don't know," I reply in an equally hushed tone. "But I can't control how my body reacts around you. I've been trying since we first ran into each other at that bar."

She moves aside the things she brought me and comes to stand beside me by the kitchen counter.

"Maybe we just need to do it once," she murmurs, slowly leaning into me. "You know, so we can take the edge off—"

I don't even give Celeste the chance to finish her sentence before I kiss her, softly and gently at first and then roughly when she returns my kiss. This time, she touches me, too, wrapping her arms around me in a warm, sensual embrace before she steps back. Keeping her eyes locked on mine, she places her hands on my hips and then slowly makes her way up to my chest, lightly tracing the word BABY—and my hardened nipples, through the fabric—with her thumbs before she pulls the sweater off above my head.

She settles into one of the kitchen bar stools and says, "Sit on my lap, Gemma baby."

I straddle her, and heat builds in my core as Celeste starts kissing me again, running her hands down my spine. Wetness pools in my underwear as she cups my face, gently but firmly, so she can kiss me deeper, longer.

Back at my friends' place, I was too desperate to touch her to think about much else. But today, I relish every single detail of her as I slowly take off her sweater, too.

"I've been wanting to do this ever since I first saw you in that restroom," I say as I run my hands over the gorgeous black flowers on the left side of her body. Now that I'm actually touching her tattoos, though, I realize that just using my hands isn't nearly enough. I take one of her hands in mine and start kissing the flowers, working my way up from her wrist, along the length of her arm, all the way to where they end below her collarbone. She arches her spine as I drag kisses up her neck and across her jaw, just the way I know she likes it.

"Gem." She bites back a moan, and I pull on her lips with my teeth.

"I love your tattoos," I say softly as I start kissing them again. "Is there any particular reason you got them?"

Her eyes half-closed with pleasure, Celeste replies, "I got them when I moved back to LA. I'd always wanted tattoos and, after the hell I went through, I thought, why not? My family hates them, since they're afraid the tattoos will scare off men."

I laugh as I start massaging her breasts. "But that's exactly what you want."

She moans, loudly and unmistakably this time, and even more so when I undo her bra and take one of her nipples into my mouth. She's writhing with pleasure by the time I've moved on to the other one.

"Bed," she says. "Now."

In her bedroom, we crash into each other, kissing ravenously like we're drowning and can't get enough air. Back in college, Celeste was always the one to take the lead in the bedroom, the one who called all the shots. But today, when she tries to push me onto the bed, I pull her so she falls with me.

I haven't had sex with another woman in eight years, but I want her, *need her*, too much to feel self-conscious about messing up. I get on top of her, grinding myself against her body.

Celeste's eyes go wide with surprise. "Gem."

Her voice is hushed, almost reverent, as I cup both of her breasts in my hands. "Fuck, I'm so wet for you. Touch me, please."

With a smirk, I slide one hand down her body and into her now soaked underwear. The moment I touch the wetness between her legs, we both moan, her because of my fingers and me because of the deep satisfaction that this is how much she wants me.

I find her clit and start moving my hand side to side, slowly at first and then faster until she's arching her back again. When she looks like she can't take it anymore, I put my fingers inside her and curl them until...

She cries out, and I hold her tight, kissing her neck, her lips, and finally her forehead as her entire body shakes.

"God," she says, slowly sitting up. "Where did you learn how to do *that*?"

"You know, the usual. Porn, romance books...but I also had a good teacher, way back when," I reply, pointedly meeting her gaze.

"Oh yeah? Speaking of which..." A mischievous look crosses Celeste's face as she moves down to my waist. When she pulls down my underwear, I'm not surprised to see it's completely soaked through. "My turn."

That's the last thing I remember before her tongue flicks my core.

Celeste

Celeste can't get enough of Gemma. That much was always true, when they were still together, at least. But there's something profoundly sexier about almost-thirty Gemma, who is so confident and *aggressive* in a way college Gemma never was.

Sure, Celeste always loved pleasuring Gemma, but in the past, Gemma tended to be more of a pillow princess, always receiving without reciprocating. And other than her quiet gasps and moans, she barely showed any signs that she was enjoying what Celeste was doing.

Celeste didn't mind it much at the time, but after Gemma quickly replaced her with someone else, it haunted her for years. In her darkest, most paranoid moments, she wondered if everything had been one-sided, after all.

But now, Celeste has no doubt that Gemma wants her,

with her own legs still lightly trembling as Gemma moans loudly, her fingers pulling on Celeste's hair. Compared to how shy and reserved she was in the past, *this* Gemma is a sex goddess, unabashedly expressing her pleasure as Celeste eats her out.

It's quite possibly the hottest thing Celeste has ever seen.

"Celeste," Gemma pants. "I'm so close. Celeste, I'm going to—"

With a loud cry, Gemma comes, her eyes rolling back as her body shakes from head to toe.

A smile threatening to overtake her lips, Celeste comes back up to lie side by side with Gemma. They kiss for a few more minutes before Gemma's eyes slowly flutter closed.

Celeste smirks. Back in college, she used to tease Gemma for always falling asleep after she climaxed. It was one of her quirks, something that *has* remained the same after all these years.

Celeste watches Gemma sleep for a moment, marveling at how much she resembles Sleeping Beauty with her gorgeous brown waves of hair spooling around her shoulders. And then, she forces herself to get out of the bed.

As she removes her makeup and contacts in front of the bathroom mirror, Celeste realizes she has no idea where things now stand between her and Gemma. They're not exactly friends, but they're not exactly exes or lovers, either. They're somewhere in between, without officially being friends with benefits.

It's all very confusing, but Celeste is admittedly glad

that Gemma passed out before they could talk about things now. It's late, and she's exhausted. Any conversation will have to wait until tomorrow.

It's only the first day of the new year, and already so much has happened between her and her ex.

25

Gemma

The next morning, I'm oddly at peace. Even with my eyes closed, I feel the pleasant warmth of sunlight pouring through the curtains. A gentle weight presses against me, making me feel safe and secure. I don't remember pulling out my weighted blanket from my box last night, but maybe I did when I was still half-asleep.

I reach down to pull my blanket off and stifle a scream when my hands make contact with *human skin*. I open my eyes to find that it's not a blanket on top of me, but a very naked Celeste.

That's when it all comes back to me. Going to the office NYE party with my ex. Coming back to her place and touching Celeste in ways I've only dreamt of doing before. *Her*, touching me, pleasuring me like she did all those years ago.

I always pass out after sex, so I guess I shouldn't have

been surprised that I never got a chance to use the toiletries that Celeste graciously provided. Meanwhile, Celeste always makes sure to remove her makeup and shower before bed, so I'm not surprised to see that her face is bare. She also always sleeps naked—or at least, she did after we started becoming intimate with one another back in college—so that's not a real surprise, either.

Feeling grimy and icky from last night, I'm thinking of how best to slip out from underneath Celeste to take a shower, when I catch sight of her face. Fast asleep, she looks peaceful in a way she normally doesn't, appearing softer and younger without her makeup.

A part of me still feels the same serenity I see on her face, but I'm also horrified at how content I feel. Why does this all still feel so nice, eight years after we last had sex? Like I'm *supposed* to wake up every morning with Celeste?

It's the hormones, I reason with myself. *Women release oxytocin, which makes us want to couple with whomever we sleep with.*

And all these hormones would have been perfectly fine if Celeste and I were dating again. But of course, that's not what's going on between us at all. Not only am I currently not looking for anything serious, but also, Celeste Min doesn't "do relationships" anymore.

Plus, she's going back to LA in a couple of weeks, since we're already down to our last set of interviews.

I groan, wondering if this is what happened to Gretchen, too. From Celeste's Instagram, they clearly worked together before they started dating. Or maybe they casually dated *while* working together. Whatever the case, the end result was the same. Celeste warned her that she didn't do relationships. Gretchen caught feelings anyway. And Celeste broke her heart.

I can easily see myself falling into that same trap of *feelings* if I don't nip it in the bud, right here and right now. I'd rather step on a pile of cat diarrhea than get that same "I don't do relationships, remember?" talk that Gretchen got from Celeste.

After managing to successfully shimmy out of bed without waking her up, I grab the toiletries from the kitchen counter and hop into the shower.

The water's freezing cold at first, causing me to yelp out loud. It's exactly the type of wake-up call I need, though, and I'm finally able to clear my head as I wash off last night's dried sweat and makeup. *And* the smell of Celeste on my skin.

I'm so focused on showering that I only realize I don't have a change of clothes until *after* I've dried myself off. Well, besides the pink pajamas Celeste gave me last night. Which I definitely am not wearing now.

After a few panicked seconds of trying to figure out what to do, I wrap the wet towel around me and exit the bathroom.

Celeste's awake by the time I walk back into her room. She's always been a light sleeper, so the sound of the shower must have woken her up. Rubbing the sleep out of her eyes, she gives me an amused look as she says, "Well, good morning. It's still early. I can make us breakfast if you want?"

She sounds so relaxed, like it's perfectly normal for me to

be in her bedroom like this. Like it's normal for us to have fucked last night, instead of it being the first time we did so in *eight years*. It's like "casual" is her middle name.

How is she so good *at this?* I want to growl in frustration as I think back to poor Gretchen throwing up in the restroom.

"Thanks, but I should head home," I say, keeping my tone light and airy. *Two* can play this game. "Happy New Year!"

I walk back to the kitchen and grab my ugly Christmas sweater from the floor.

Still completely naked, Celeste rolls over so she's propped up on her elbows. Her long legs in the air behind her, she stares at me with those gorgeously dark eyes of hers.

A puzzled expression scrunches up her face before smoothing out into acceptance.

"Gem," she says. "Let me at least lend you a change of clothes so you don't have to wear what you wore yesterday. Like what you did for me last time."

Borrowing a change of clothes from Celeste would mean that I'd have to smell like her again. I'm about to tell her no thanks, when her face lights up with an idea.

"Oh, I still have that shirt you let me borrow last time," she says. "I washed it for you and everything. Let me go get it."

She gets up from the bed, and I get a full, unavoidable view of her bare chest. *How the heck did I sleep with those breasts pressed up against me for the entire night?*

I want to ask her if she can put some clothes on, but also, if I'm being honest with myself, I kind of don't.

She fishes out my shirt from the closet and hands it to

me. I sniff it warily and breathe a small sigh of relief when it smells like generic, citrusy laundry detergent.

I gladly put it on.

I'm less lucky on the underwear front, because the bikini briefs I wore yesterday are a complete mess. I don't dare wear them again, unwashed. I fold them up and stash them in my purse.

Well, at least my pants are still wearable. Going commando isn't exactly how I thought I'd start off the New Year, but I don't have a choice.

I'm slipping on my pants when Celeste says, "Let me drop you off at your friends' place."

"It's okay," I say. "I was thinking of taking public transportation."

She shakes her head. "The train schedule is weird today because of the holiday. Here, if you don't want me to drive, I can get a car for you," she says, holding up her phone. "If I request it now, your driver will arrive in around eight minutes. Is that enough time for you?"

"More than enough. Thanks."

While we wait, Celeste finally goes to her closet and pulls on a long, black pajama T-shirt. She folds her arms across her chest, and we wordlessly stare at each other until my ride arrives.

My head still spinning from everything that happened in the last twelve hours, I don't let myself fully relax until I'm in the car, on the way back home.

26

Celeste

When she woke up on New Year's Day to find Gemma standing in her bedroom with nothing but a towel wrapped around herself, Celeste almost broke her own rules.

The sight was too intimately familiar, like the Gemma from eight years ago had somehow time traveled to the present day. Back when they used to live together in their crappy LA apartment, the bathroom mirror would always fog up, so both she and Gemma would have to wrap themselves up in their towels and change in the bedroom, instead. Even though it was an inconvenience brought on by the misfortune of being broke college students, this and other quiet, mundane moments with Gemma were some of Celeste's fondest memories.

Fortunately, the current Gemma had refused Celeste's

offer to cook breakfast, pulling her back to the cold reality of the present. *If she hadn't, well…*

Back in her bed, Celeste stops herself from thinking about might haves and would haves. Instead, she forces herself to, not for the first time, think about *what is* and *what isn't.*

She and Gemma had fun at the party last night. That is a fact. Then they came back to her place and had sex. Also a fact.

Despite all this, the morning after, Gemma couldn't get away from her fast enough. Celeste had tried her best to be calm and relaxed, hoping that would help them get everything sorted out this morning. But maybe it'd been for the best that they didn't. After all, Celeste doesn't do relationships. Not anymore. She can't completely forget that because of one tender moment of nostalgia.

Although they're exes, Celeste still cares about Gemma. She doesn't want to hurt her again.

Back when they seriously dated in college, Celeste believed that the happily-ever-afters she grew up reading about were real. When she and Gemma just *happened* to become roommates at the beginning of junior year, and then they just *happened* to become so much more than that, Celeste thought that she was finally getting a love story of her own.

But then, of course, *real* life had taken everything away from her. Just like that.

Her mother had believed in love stories, too. In fact, she's the reason why Celeste had fallen in love with romantic

K-dramas and other love stories to begin with. But after witnessing what her mother went through all those years ago *and* experiencing her own heartbreak with Gemma, Celeste had realized another probable fact. As entertaining as they are, love stories simply aren't real. Or at least, for some unknown reason, they aren't real for people like her and her mother. And there's no use in believing otherwise.

Celeste only has one more set of interviews with Gemma. After that, they'll return to their normal, separate lives in LA and SF, respectively. And she'll finally be able to move on from the past.

Celeste's alarm goes off, ripping her away from her thoughts. She reaches her arm out to turn off the incessant beeping and gets a whiff of Gemma's scent, her eyes fluttering closed at the pleasant aroma. Before she can stop herself, she's scooped up the blanket and gathered it up in her hands, sniffing it like some drug addict. Somehow, Gemma smells even better than she remembers.

Celeste thinks back to a study she discovered online that found that lesbian women and straight men react similarly to women's pheromones in a way that straight women do not. At a time when everyone around her was denying her existence—or said "there was something wrong" with her—studies like this had made her feel a bit better.

"See?" she'd tell her parents. "There's a scientific reason why I like girls. I'm just built different!"

Of course, now she knows better, and that no one has to have *any* reason, scientific or otherwise, to be gay. But it seemed to placate her parents enough, or at least until

Celeste reached her twenties and the "you should find a nice husband and have kids" conversations started.

Celeste *does* want kids. Just not the husband.

Before she gets out of bed again, Celeste scrolls through the notifications on her phone, in case she somehow missed a message or a call from her mother. It's something she's been doing every morning since she moved back to LA, since Korea is seventeen hours ahead of California.

But today, there's only a message from Min-joon. Nothing from her mother. And no news is good news. She lets out a quiet sigh of relief.

Eight years ago, she'd checked her phone and found out she had a missed call from her mom. And when she'd called her mother back, that one single phone conversation had completely upended her life. Her stomach twists into knots just thinking about it.

She sneaks one last whiff of Gemma before throwing her bedding in the washing machine. Then, after starting the cycle and turning on the coffee machine, she opens the windows.

The cool, salty air chills her face, and she takes a deep breath.

Just one more set of interviews. She can do this.

27

Gemma

The first few days of the new year go by without a single word from Celeste. This isn't *that* abnormal, coming from her. But this time, things feel different. This time, it really does feel like we should talk about what happened between us, before we do our last set of interviews.

We probably should have talked on New Year's, but I've never been good at processing things as they happen. And neither has Celeste, or at least, not when we were in college. In the few times we fought while we dated, we'd always leave each other alone for a couple of days to mull things over before trying to resolve anything.

Now that I've had some time and space, though, I'm ready to talk. But I don't even know how to begin. After all, I'm entirely to blame this time. I'm the one who invited her to the company holiday party. And I'm the one who quite literally put my fingers inside of her.

Well, she more than returned the favor afterward. But I'm the one that first took us to that level, going way past just kissing or making out.

I do my usual song and dance of writing an email to Celeste and deleting it. In the end, it's Evelyn who breaks the ice for us, cc'ing both Celeste and me before I leave the office on the first Friday of the year.

From: evelynsanderson@citrine.com
To: gemmacho@citrine.com
CC: celeste@celestemin.com
Subject: Last Set of Interviews

Hi, ladies. We're ready to start on our final interview segment. We're still searching for the second couple, but for now, I'd like you to interview Rob and Marge Roy. They're in their 80s so be gentle with them, please. But hopefully things will still be fun.

She's attached the couple's contact information at the bottom of the email.

I smile, thinking back to my grandparents, who passed away when I was younger but were very much in love with each other until their dying day.

"I can't stand this old man," my grandma would always say in Korean whenever we visited her. But it'd always be with a slight smile on her lips, one that widened when the two of them walked hand in hand around their neighborhood park, talking about how cute the ducks were or what so-and-so said in their *hwatu* card-playing circle last week. During these walks with my grandparents, Kid Me would always rush ahead of them after loudly declaring, "Halmoni and Harabeoji are too slow!"

But then I would look back at them and dream about a time when I'd also find that kind of love.

I'm still thinking about my grandma and grandpa when I realize that, even though I had plenty of examples in my life of heteroromantic happy couples, I never had examples of happy *sapphic* couples growing up. I wonder if I would have realized I'm bi sooner if I were exposed to couples like Val and Kiara when I was a kid.

I'm still brainstorming everything when I hop in the shower back at my friends' apartment. The weather in San Francisco has been cold and misty lately, as it typically is during this time of year, so my tense body is dying for some hot water to relax my muscles. In the pleasant warmth, I close my eyes and thoroughly massage my temples until I feel refreshed enough to tackle the tasks I have left to do today.

When I get out of the shower, I do two things: (1) I email Rob and Marge to ask when would be the most convenient time for them to come in for an interview, and (2) I send Celeste a message on KakaoTalk.

Hey, do you want to meet up sometime before the final interview? I think we have a lot to unpack after what happened on New Year's. And I'd like us to talk about an idea I have, too.

Celeste responds instantly with, Sure. Brunch tomorrow?

I'm surprised by her suggestion, because the Celeste *I* know is *not* a brunch person. Back in college, she always just came along with me because she knew I liked it.

It'd have been sweet that she suggested it...if we were still dating.

Maybe she's just being polite. Or maybe she likes brunch now.

Trying my best not to think much of it, I send her some recommended spots and set up a time to meet.

Gemma

I meet Celeste at an Asian dessert café on Octavia Street, far away from *both* our places. After what happened the last time Celeste and I met up at a coffeehouse, I know better than to pick somewhere out of convenience.

Today, Celeste is wearing mahogany brown frames that, along with her sleek, formfitting gray turtleneck sweater dress, make her look like some ingenious, sexy architect rather than the photographer she really is.

I barely resist the urge to circle my arm around her waist as we enter the building.

Despite only opening fifteen minutes ago, the café is already crowded with couples and college students. Its interior is a cute white and pink, with lightbulbs encased in clear spheres hanging down from the ceiling. Along with the small houseplants on gold shelves and multicolored plastic chairs, the place looks adorable enough to be in a

K-drama. Even the menu on the wall is highly aesthetically pleasing, with a pink backdrop and white all-caps letters.

"Wow," I say, looking around in wonder. "This café is even prettier than it looked in the pictures."

"Yeah, thanks for suggesting it, Gem," Celeste replies, giving me a small smile.

Her shoulders are tense, and so are mine.

I clear my throat. "We should find a seat and order first. You know. Before we talk."

"Right."

I choose a table by the wall that has white-framed pictures of various Asian desserts.

"I know you don't like traditional American brunch," I say. "So I only suggested places that were a bit more unique."

Celeste's eyes widen. She looks away, her cheeks turning a little red. "Thanks."

"No problem! I love dessert places, too, so..." I clear my throat again and pick up the clipboard menu from the table.

I'm instantly overwhelmed by the countless varieties of shaved ice, milk tea drinks, and baked goods. It takes me a few minutes to come to a decision.

"I think I'll go with the milk tea *bingsu*," I say.

"And I'll get the mango sticky rice crepe," Celeste replies with only a cursory glance at the menu.

I bite the inside of my cheek. Celeste has always loved mangoes.

Although very cute, the café is unfortunately a bit cramped, with small gaps between the tables. From where

I'm sitting with my back against the wall, I can't get out unless Celeste moves first.

"Here," Celeste says, noticing my predicament. "I'll go order for us."

I hand her the menu, and she goes up to the register to order our food. With her back turned toward me, I follow the lines of her shoulders, down to her hourglass figure, and then to much lower than I'd normally be comfortable staring.

Whispers come from a nearby table. A few college-aged boys sneak glances at Celeste, laughing and murmuring among themselves. They're obviously talking about her, and I stand up from my seat, ready to parkour across the table and fight them if they start catcalling her.

But I worried for nothing, because at that moment, Celeste finishes ordering and fixes them with a steely glare. From where I'm sitting, I can't hear what she says, but whatever it is, it's apparently enough to make them all blush and leave the café.

"What did you say to those boys?" I ask Celeste when she sits back down at our table.

"Don't worry about it," she replies with a mischievous smile. "Let's just say they'll think twice before blatantly staring at a woman like that again."

I look down at my feet, suddenly embarrassed. Because of course, I was also ogling Celeste. I'm no better than the boys.

"What?" Celeste asks. "Why do you have that weird look on your face?"

I sigh. I've always been a bad liar, so I don't even try. "I was thinking that I'm no better than those boys. Because I was doing the exact same thing. That's why I wanted to meet you. I can't help myself around you. No matter how much I try to keep things professional."

Celeste bites her lip, and my attention immediately flickers to her mouth before going up to her eyes again. She's staring at me, too, like I'm the only other person in this café.

The café's cute, calming atmosphere does little to slow down my heartbeat.

"Gem," she says in a low voice. "You're definitely better than the boys."

"And why is that?"

"Because I *want* you to stare at me. And I don't think I can keep things professional with you, either. Especially not after New Year's." She coughs and looks away. "I actually thought of asking you if you want to 'officially' be friends with benefits."

Before I can even think about how to respond, our food arrives. We awkwardly sit there with everything she said lingering in the air around us as the server sets the plates down on our table.

When he leaves, Celeste continues, "But I know you don't do casual. So I didn't."

I stare down at the food in front of me. Everything looks so delicious, brightly colored and glistening in the warm, yellow light. My bingsu is literally drowning in condensed milk. So good, yet so bad.

"I'm actually not looking for anything serious right now," I say, meeting Celeste's eyes. "Don't get me wrong. I still value relationships. But after what happened with my ex-fiancé, I don't think I'm in the right place for anything serious. So I'm down to have some fun. As long as it doesn't interfere with the project."

I scoop a spoonful of bingsu into my mouth as a little self-reward for finally telling Celeste what I want. It melts in my mouth, so good that my eyes roll to the back of my head. When I look up from the dessert, Celeste is staring at me, her mouth slightly open. Her gaze slides down to my lips, her eyes growing dark and wanting.

My mouth feels sticky, and I dab my lips with a napkin. Sure enough, the cloth comes back with blotches of cream. Before I can stop her, Celeste reaches over and runs her thumb across my lips.

"Here," she says. "You missed a spot." Her gentle yet possessive tone makes a shiver run down my spine.

"So," I say when I'm able to speak again. "What do you say?"

Celeste takes a bite of her crepe, looking deep in thought as she chews. I have some more of my own dessert, keeping my eyes on my bowl this time.

After she swallows, she finally says, "I'm down to see you casually, too. But only if you're okay with the fact that I'm returning to LA once we finish the project. And I don't know when I'll next come up north."

Even though it's not a surprise, my heart squeezes at the very thought of Celeste leaving again. But I shoo that feeling away. We're going to have fun. That's all.

"Sounds good," I say. "Speaking of the project, we should also talk about the next interview."

"Of course."

"I know Evelyn wants us to interview Rob and Marge, but what do you think about also interviewing a sapphic elderly couple?" I ask. "Because I don't know about you, but when I was growing up, I hardly saw any older queer women. On TV or in person."

Celeste sits up in her seat. "I didn't grow up seeing *any* queer elders in Korea," she says. "Not any that were out, anyway. So I think that's an excellent idea. Do you think Evelyn will approve?"

"Knowing her, she most likely will. I remember reading an article once about how young queer people are more likely to... harm themselves because they don't think they can have happily-ever-afters. While hetero couples get that kind of representation all the time."

I apparently struck a nerve, because Celeste grows extremely still.

"Yeah, I think this interview will be great," she says quietly. "Maybe we can also try to find a non-white couple for this last interview. Since Rob and Marge are white and so were Aaron and Brent."

By the time we finish our food, I've sent Evelyn an email detailing everything.

"We work well together, Gem," Celeste remarks as we exit the café. From her low, sultry tone, I know she doesn't mean just professionally.

Her lips are centimeters away from mine when I reply, “We always have.”

But before we can kiss, my phone buzzes in my pocket. Celeste steps back so I can get out my phone and check the notification.

“It’s Evelyn,” I tell Celeste. “She loves our idea. She’s going to use her contacts to find an older sapphic couple for us.”

“That’s great! I’m looking forward to this next set of interviews.”

We pause and burst out laughing. It’s amazing how we can so easily switch gears from sexy to professional.

One moment, we’re smiling at each other, and in the next, Celeste is kissing me, long and deep. She only pauses to whisper in my ear, “I don’t know if I’ve ever told you this, but you have beautiful, irresistible lips.”

Suddenly, the sugar from the bingsu isn’t the only thing giving me a high. My heart beats faster and louder, so much that I wonder if Celeste can hear it, too. She says something else, and it takes me a moment to process her words.

My voice comes out breathy and quiet when I ask, “Wait, what?”

“I said, do you want to go back to my place?” she repeats herself, flashing me an amused grin.

“Oh, God, yes,” I say. “I’m so turned on right now.”

Celeste smiles and gives me a peck on the lips. “Okay, let’s go.”

On our way back to her place, I send my friends a text: So, Celeste and I agreed to be in a casual relationship together. Like, officially.

Kiara is the first to reply. I KNEW you two wouldn't be able to stay professional for long!

"Casual"? Val asks. And how are you feeling about that?

Good, actually! I reply. Taking your advice from way back when to let things flow the way they're going.

Val sends back a thumbs-up that makes me giggle. She even texts like a Boomer sometimes.

Have fun and have lots of sex! Kiara replies. Don't come back home tonight! K THANKS LOVE YOU BYE!!!!

Val sends a stream of crying-while-laughing emojis, and I grin.

~

Celeste and I barely make it back to her place before we start taking each other's clothes off. She still tastes sugary-sweet from the dessert, so I can't keep my mouth off hers as we move to her bed.

Celeste puts a pillow under my pelvis, propping me up before running her hands up my legs and around my hips. My back arches when her mouth finds my center, and she chuckles as my breaths come out in light gasps.

"Yes," I murmur. "Just like that."

She reaches up to cup my breasts, massaging them as her tongue flicks at my core. Heat builds up in my center, and I'm about to come when she suddenly sits up.

"Wha—" But before I can say anything else, she's sucking on my nipples, making shivers run down my spine. She leaves a trail of kisses from my chest to the folds between my legs.

I'm writhing now, breathless moans coming out of my mouth as her tongue swirls and licks at my clit.

"You always taste so good," Celeste says as she readjusts her grip on my hips.

"Don't stop. I'm so close."

Celeste inserts a finger into me, then two, keeping pace with the flicks of her tongue. All the pleasure that's built up inside me explodes into my release. When I catch my breath, an idea pops into my head. It's not something I'm *super* confident about doing, but I want to try it, regardless.

My voice comes out in a whisper when I say, "Celeste, I want to taste you."

29

Celeste

Celeste blinks up at Gemma, her thoughts whirring as she processes her words. "You do?"

"Yeah. I never got the chance before we..." Gemma trails off and bites her lip, and Celeste's heart beats faster from how adorable she looks. "I've always wanted to, but back in college, I was too intimidated to try. And if I'm being honest, I'm still scared. Fingers, I could figure out. But my mouth? I don't know."

Celeste gently kisses Gemma on her forehead. "Why don't you just try it, then? If you want me to, I can let you know how you're doing and guide you through it."

Gemma's eyes widen, her breaths noticeably quickening.

"I don't expect you to be amazing, Gem," Celeste reassures her. "So don't worry. And I really do want this. Just talking about it is making me wet again."

A smile finally returns to Gemma's lips. "Okay, I'll try it."

At first, she's too eager, the movements of her tongue rough and hard.

"Easy," Celeste hisses, gently running her fingers through Gemma's long hair before gathering it up with her hands. "Try a bit less pressure. Also, next time, we should have a hair tie ready for you."

Gemma nods before slowly resuming her licking, more gently this time as she starts flicking her tongue up and down from Celeste's entrance to her clit.

Celeste gasps. Gemma is catching on. Slowly but surely.

It takes a few more experimental licks in various directions and instructions from Celeste, but all the waiting and guidance proves worth it when Gemma finally figures it out. Hot, delicious warmth builds up inside Celeste, and she can barely think straight when Gemma adds her fingers into the mix.

"Gem," Celeste pants. "Gem, that's it. Right there. I'm going to—"

She cries out, and Gemma eagerly laps at her wetness.

"You taste so good," she says. "Holy shit. It's better than I imagined it'd be."

When Gemma comes back up, Celeste is still breathless. "See?" she says when she can finally talk. "You just had to try it out for yourself."

"Yeah," replies Gemma. "Sorry it took so long, though."

Celeste gives her forehead another kiss. "Nah, you were fine."

For a moment, they stay like that, lying side by side while staring into each other's eyes. Celeste's heart flutters, and not from the recent orgasm.

"Why don't I make us some dinner?" Celeste asks, getting out of bed. "I don't know about you, but I'm hungry, maybe because we didn't eat a proper lunch."

Gemma clears her throat. Celeste holds her breath, and she half-expects Gemma to say she has to go home again. But then, Gemma sits up and says, "Sounds good. Anything I can do to help?"

At long last, Celeste lets herself relax. "No," she says with a mischievous grin. "You just stay in my bed like that, naked and sexy."

Gemma

Celeste makes us not only dinner, but also breakfast the next morning, brewing us steaming hot coffee and expertly making fancy Korean street toast that I've only had in LA Koreatown cafés.

As I bite into my sandwich stuffed with veggie omelet, cheese, and sausage, I can't help but think of Val and Kiara and how they started dating. Celeste's and my situation couldn't be more different than theirs, but my heart beats faster, regardless.

"What do you have going on for the rest of the weekend?" Celeste asks with her hands wrapped around her coffee mug.

I blink. Since the holidays are over now and I have everything sorted out for my move later in the month, I don't have any plans. I was planning on taking it easy and maybe watch an episode—or five—of a new rom-com K-drama I've seen people talk about online.

When I tell this to Celeste, she gasps.

"Oh, I've been wanting to watch that, too," she says, clapping her hands. "I don't have much going on today, either. Want to watch it together?"

"Sure."

I've only seen Celeste clap her hands excitedly in one context: when we're talking about cute K-dramas. The unexpected flash of familiarity makes me grin.

After we finish eating and cleaning up our plates, Celeste and I return to her bedroom. She steps out momentarily and comes back with her laptop and bed tray table, the same one she had when we were in college. Then, we cuddle up in bed together and hit play.

The show is cute, albeit a tad bit stereotypical with its standard poor-girl-meets-the-rich-son-of-the-CEO K-drama plot. The overarching story has more to it than that, but Celeste and I don't get past the first couple of episodes before we're kissing again.

Finally, Celeste places the tray table down on the floor.

"Let's finish the rest later," she says while kissing down my neck.

With a sharp inhale, I nod. Then, I gently place a hand below her chin and guide her lips back to mine.

The K-drama thankfully ends up being a lot more entertaining than I thought it'd be, but if someone asked me what the show is about, I wouldn't be able to tell them.

Most of my focus is on Celeste and learning and relearning how she reacts to me touching different areas of her body. She more than returns the favor, and I consider myself lucky I'm even able to show up to work on Monday.

At lunch, Val takes one look at my disheveled state and says to Kiara, "Ah, young love. Babe, remember when we were like that?"

Kiara laughs. "What are you talking about? We're still like that."

I widen my eyes. After making sure no one is within earshot in the café, I hiss, "You guys still have this much sex?"

Val scrunches up her nose. "Well... it comes and goes in waves. We haven't been able to do much while you're around, for example, but now... let's just say that Burrito's been sleeping in the living room."

"Oh God," I laugh. "I'm so sorry. Good thing I'm moving out in a couple of weeks."

"Speaking of which," says Kiara. "You've thoroughly vetted your new place, right? Because I don't want you to accidentally move into some secret meth lab or something equally sketchy."

Both Val and I give Kiara a surprised look.

"How in the world did you come up with *that* scenario?" Val asks in horror.

Kiara laughs. "Sorry, I've been rewatching *Breaking Bad* on my tablet while you game."

"*Re*watching?" Val exclaims. "Just when I thought I

couldn't love you any more. I had no idea you liked that shit! Oh man, we're watching *Metástasis* together next."

"*Metástasis*?" I ask.

"It's the Colombian remake of *Breaking Bad*. Not everyone likes it, but... I think it's pretty good."

Val and Kiara end up talking about TV shows for the rest of lunch while I go through my emails. One of them is a message from Evelyn saying she found an older sapphic couple for us to interview. By the end of the workday, we've scheduled the last two interviews for "Modern Love in Focus" this coming Saturday, one in the morning and one in the afternoon.

After I leave the office, Celeste and I meet up at an indie bookstore near the Golden Gate Park.

"It's good that we're doing this. A nice little break from just being holed up in my apartment," Celeste says with a grin as we enter through the door.

I'd originally planned on visiting the store by myself to buy a couple books to help with advice requests that'd come in recently for Dear Karl. But Celeste asked to tag along, saying she's been meaning to pick up some photography books for a while now.

I've always loved bookstores, and my good mood is only amplified by the comforting smell of old books. The store's high ceilings and brightly colored walls are a huge bonus, and I find myself humming cheerfully as I browse the shelves. As we walk around together, Celeste smiles and points out various fun-looking books.

Even though I'm technically here for work, I can't help but sneak glances at Celeste, observing how the overhead lights of the store reflect in her deep, dark eyes. I think I'm being sneaky, but a few minutes later, she meets my gaze and smiles. "What?"

"Just looking," I say.

Her grin widens. "For books or at me?"

"Both."

"Uh-huh. Find anything interesting?"

I hold up the book about breakups I'd been carrying in the crook of my arm.

Celeste reads the title with raised eyebrows. "Ouch, are you thinking of ending things with me already?" she asks in an obviously joking tone.

I laugh. "Please. We'd have to be in a relationship for me to do that. It's for work. A lot of people broke up over the holidays and wrote in to our column. I usually know what to say, but I like to read books like this from time to time, so I can have more ideas on how to handle certain situations."

"Makes sense," Celeste replies with a nod.

We don't say much else after that, and at some point, we even drift away from each other to look at different sections. But instead of being awkward, everything feels natural, like we're two boats drifting closer and farther away from each other with the gentle ebb and flow of the tide.

I'm still browsing books when Celeste approaches me again, carrying a large stack.

"I think I'm done," she says. "Ready to go whenever you are, but no rush."

Curious, I peer down at the books in her hands. Most of them are about photography, but there are also a couple of pink and yellow books at the bottom that catch my eye.

I freeze. "Are those romance novels? You still like those?"

Celeste's face reddens. "Yup."

My brain short-circuits. "How—what—"

I don't continue my train of thought. I can barely process the fact that present-day "I don't do relationships" Celeste Min still likes *romance books.*

"Hm?" Celeste says.

"Don't get me wrong," I say slowly. "There's nothing wrong with liking them. But..."

"But?"

I hesitate, trying my best to form my confusion into words. "How can someone who still loves romance novels so much... be so against relationships?"

"Romance books are fiction," Celeste replies with a shrug. "They're products of an author's brain and have no basis in real life. They're predictable, and there's always a happy ending. Real relationships, though? Not as nice and a lot messier."

She shudders, like there's a sudden chill.

"And why do you believe that?" I ask, realizing I never directly asked her this question. Without meaning to, I've put my advice columnist hat on, fascinated to finally get a peek inside Celeste's head.

She stares at me for a long moment, as if she's trying to decide what to say. Finally, she looks down at the books in her hands. "Come on, Gem. Would you still believe in romance if you were me? After the shit show that's my parents' relationship? And after what happened to us?"

I squeeze my books to my chest. "Us?"

She glances around, as if checking to see if the coast is clear. I do the same. We have pretty much the entire section to ourselves.

Quietly, Celeste continues, "You were my last girlfriend. My last real relationship. I never got over what happened with us. And how fast you moved on."

The entire way back to Celeste's apartment, I stay silent. I can't even look at her face. My heart's hurting too much.

I think back to how *I* was eight years ago, when Celeste's and my breakup was still fresh. Since I had no idea *what* had happened to Celeste or *why* she'd left, I didn't know how to cope. I took her disappearance so personally, especially since she didn't reply to any of my messages. I really thought she just didn't want to be around me anymore, so I was desperate to find someone who did, going to parties every weekend and hooking up with anyone who gave me the time of day. Like Celeste, I didn't even *want* to seriously date again. Until I met James at one of the last parties I went to in college.

Despite the laughably tragic end of our relationship, when we met, James helped me believe in love again, making me laugh when I thought I couldn't and holding me tight whenever I cried. He made me feel so safe and wanted that I didn't even hesitate when he asked me to be his girlfriend. And when we moved seven hours up north from LA to SF, he made the transition from college to the real world so fun and easy.

James may be an asshole, but he's an asshole I'll always owe a lot to. I try to imagine a world where I *hadn't* met him. Would I have completely given up on relationships, too?

But of course, no amount of gratitude can surpass what I know now. About James and me. And about Celeste. I'm so caught up with all my different thoughts and emotions that I don't realize we're back at Celeste's place until I bump into her as she unlocks the door.

When we're back inside, Celeste says, "Gem. Sorry, maybe I shouldn't have told you all that."

I shake my head. My voice comes out soft and hoarse when I reply, "No, I'm glad you did. It's given me a lot to think about."

Celeste gives me a quizzical look. "How so?"

My eyes burn with tears. "I know we agreed that we both fucked up," I say. "But for what it's worth, I'm really sorry, Celeste. I wish I'd waited longer for you. I wish we lived in an alternative universe where we're still together here in SF."

Her eyes widen, and she looks at me for a long moment before wiping the drops on my cheeks. "It was such a long time ago, Gem," she says. "We were both young and could have handled the situation a lot better. Come on, let's not talk about sad stuff anymore. I'm glad we cleared the air a bit more, but I'm so sick of being sad. And I can use a pick-me-up."

She pulls me in close, and I start kissing her, slowly moving down her neck and to the rest of her body. I can't change what happened in the past, but I *can* change how she feels at this very moment.

"In that case," I say. "Let me be of service."

31

Celeste

In the week before their last shoot, Celeste wakes up every day kissing Gemma in the morning and goes to sleep with her arms around her every night. It's like she died and went to heaven, except her heaven has always been the too-brief time in college when she and Gemma lived together.

She can't remember the last time she laughed so much, can't remember the last time she was this *happy*. It's a dangerous type of joy. One that's so overwhelming she feels like she's floating, seconds away from crashing back down to the ground.

Every little moment she spends with Gemma feels so precious, to the point that Celeste finds herself unable to sleep in the first few hours of Thursday morning. She watches Gemma as she sleeps, gently running her fingers through the other woman's long, wavy hair.

It's been a few days, but she can't stop thinking about how Gemma had cried for her and the past they'll never be able to undo. The emotion in her voice had been so raw and genuine that Celeste's own heart ached.

That's what she's always loved about Gemma. From the moment they met during their junior year, she's always been so earnest. So sincere. While Celeste herself spends most of her time trying *not* to care, Gemma is the opposite, caring so deeply about everything and everyone.

And that's exactly why, despite her own rekindled feelings for Gemma, Celeste knows she can't stay in her ex's life. Even though Gemma claimed she's not looking for anything serious, Celeste *knows* her. The casual relationship thing is most likely a phase, brought on by how badly she was fucked up by her most recent relationship.

It's only a matter of time before Gemma will want something more serious. And after all she's been through, she deserves someone who can be one hundred percent sure about her and give her the future, the *relationship*, she wants. And that's not Celeste.

Celeste knows all that, but she can't help but wish she can stretch this week out as long as she can. They now only have three days left of this project. Three days that she wants to enjoy with Gemma to the fullest before they go their separate ways.

Celeste sits up in bed and grabs her phone from the bedside drawer.

A month ago, she'd gotten an email about a short shoot in Sausalito. Since it's only for a day, and just across the

Golden Gate Bridge from where she's staying, she'd said yes without thinking too much about it. At the time, she had no idea it would be the day before her last shoot for "Modern Love in Focus."

Compared to the busy hustle and bustle of San Francisco, Sausalito is far quieter and smaller, with picturesque bayside views that end up on postcards. Previously, she'd only thought of it as another work trip. But now, it occurs to her that, if Gemma's up for it, it can easily be a mini vacation. A little getaway they can go on to celebrate finishing a project they both worked hard on.

With a groan, Gemma stirs by her side. "I passed out again, didn't I?"

Celeste laughs. "It's a little past three. Welcome to Thursday."

Gemma lets out an even louder groan. "I'm fucked. I have to get ready for work in a few hours. What if I can't go back to sleep?"

"Oh, don't you worry about that," Celeste says. She runs a hand down Gemma's spine, causing the other woman to shudder with pleasure. "I'm sure I can get you sleeping again in no time."

Gemma laughs and turns over to curiously peer down at Celeste's phone. "What are you up to? Emails? At this hour?"

"Kind of. Are you doing anything on Friday?"

"Besides work? Not really. Why?"

"I'm going up to Sausalito for another project. Do you want to come with me? It's gorgeous there, and I think it'd be a nice little trip before..." It'd seemed so easy when she thought it, but out loud, it takes Celeste a moment to go on. "Our last shoot together."

Gemma stiffens. Avoiding Celeste's gaze, she checks her own phone and asks, "What time do we have to get there by? I'll have to take some work home, but I can leave around two, so we can avoid rush hour."

"Two is perfect, since the shoot starts at three. I'll drive, and I'll pick you up from your office. I know a few cafés where you can finish up work. If you want, we could also go on a fancy dinner date by the shore at the end of the day. I'll pay for all expenses, obviously. Since it's my work trip."

"You should have led with that!" Gemma jokes. But her voice grows soft as she continues, "But yeah... that sounds like a good..." With a frown, she abruptly clears her throat. "Anyway, I'm down. Thanks for coming up with this idea. I've been needing a little getaway for a while now."

"It's no problem. I was thinking we could also stay there overnight if that's okay with you? Since our first interview the next day isn't until ten a.m. We should have plenty of time to come back down to SF."

Gemma lies back onto the bed. "Sounds good. I'll go to my friends' apartment tomorrow—or I guess *today*—after work to pack an overnight bag, then."

"All right." Celeste puts her phone away and slowly closes the distance between them. "Now that we've taken care of all that, are you ready for your nightcap?"

"Oh, yes, please."

32

Gemma

When I return to Kiara and Val's apartment on Thursday night, the lights are off, and the entire apartment is covered with candles. Burrito is nowhere to be seen, and slow, classical music plays from the TV speakers. I'm afraid I've walked into some kind of sex thing when the smell of sage wafts to my nose.

"Gemma!" Kiara says, coming out of the bedroom. She closes the door behind her and throws her arms out for a hug.

"Watch your step," Val cautions. "There are candles all over the place."

"Were you guys about to have a date night?" I ask warily, just in case. "Where's Burrito?"

"Burrito's in the bedroom, underneath our bed," Kiara answers. "He hates candles. And nah, it's several days late, I know, but we're about to do a New Year's manifestation ritual. Join us!"

Sapphics are, stereotypically, a superstitious group, but Kiara is the most into the woo out of anyone I know. She's been doing little rituals since I've known her, and Val always indulges her, even though she's not a spiritual person, herself.

"It makes her so happy when I participate," Val explained to me once. "So I can't say no."

Kiara places a yellow cushion on the floor for me so it joins the other two already there. But as I sit down, I realize I have no idea what I'm manifesting. A new job? I'm happy with my current one, and if this modern love project does well, it'll hopefully make things even better. A new relationship? I'm happy with how things are with Celeste and me. Even though it's temporary.

Stumped, I sit down on my cushion and stare into one of the candles.

Kiara starts by asking us to share what we're manifesting.

"A promotion," Val says. "They're making me do twice the amount of work I signed up for, and it's time I got better pay for it. Or find a better job, but I like working with you two, so . . . we'll see. What about you, hon?"

"A better place in the Ticketmaster queue for Beyoncé's next tour," Kiara says rapidly, like she's recited this multiple times. "Life's been good lately, but I still haven't fully recovered from us missing the *Renaissance* tour! As cool as the movie version was, I need to see my queen live and in the flesh!"

"Don't worry, babe," replies Val. "Next time, it's going to be all hands on deck. I don't care if we need to go on PTO to virtually stand in line or what, because we are *getting* the tickets before the scalpers drive up the prices." She makes a determined fist.

I feel a twinge of guilt. Trying to get tickets for the *Renaissance* tour was yet another thing I missed while I was wrapped up in my life with James.

"I'll help, too," I say. "I'll take the whole day off if I need to."

"Aw!" Kiara wraps us both in her arms. "I love you guys!"

Both my friends then turn to me.

"How about you, Gemma?" Val asks. "What are you manifesting?"

I let out a nervous laugh. "Well, I was thinking about how everything is finally good for me now, too. I'm almost done with the project for Evelyn. And my thing with Celeste—"

Kiara gasps, cutting me off. "That's right! How's that going?"

"It's been great," I reply. "I'm really happy right now. I almost wish it didn't have to end so soon."

"Soon?" Kiara says with a frown.

"Yup. We're only seeing each other until we finish this project. Afterward, Celeste is returning to LA and that'll be that."

Val leans back, folding her arms to her chest. "I know I'm the one who told you to go with the flow, but will you be okay when it all ends? You've been spending a lot of time with her recently."

"Right," Kiara says. "You seem to really like her, Gemma. And you're so happy with her! This doesn't have to be the *end* end, right? I mean, your parents live in SoCal, too! Maybe you two can do long distance!"

"Yeah," I reply. "But I don't think Celeste has any interest in continuing this. Or at least, that's the impression I got from what she's been saying."

Val and Kiara exchange worried glances.

"Honestly, after what happened with my last relationship," I continue, "I've been trying to stay in the present. I learned the hard way that sometimes it's best not to worry so much about the future. And even if this thing with Celeste doesn't go anywhere, I don't think I'll ever regret reconnecting with her. It's been super healing and helpful, since we resolved a lot of things from the past."

Kiara smiles. "Well, I'm happy for you, then. And proud of you, too! It sounds like you're in a good place." She glances around at the candles. "Okay, I have an idea. Gemma, how about for you, we manifest a new, healthy, and happy long-term relationship! Not necessarily for right now, but for somewhere along the line. Whenever you're ready!"

I make a face. "Can we do that? I thought manifesting was for things you wanted to happen in the near future."

"Not necessarily!" Kiara says. "Things might happen quickly, or they might happen years later. You never know."

Val nods. "Yeah, why not? If Kiara is manifesting tickets for a tour Beyoncé hasn't even announced yet—a tour she may have not even *planned* yet—why can't you manifest a new relationship you want at *some* point?"

Kiara giggles. "Everything happens in divine timing."

"And Beyoncé's, apparently," Val quips.

"Bitch, Beyoncé *is* a goddess!" Kiara exclaims jokingly. "What are you talking about? It's like that one Ariana Grande song. God is a woman, period."

We all cheer in agreement and join hands to start the ritual.

~

On Friday afternoon, I exit through the doors of my office building. The city streets are loud and crowded, and, at first, I'm worried Celeste won't be able to get to me. But then a white BMW zips through traffic and comes to a stop in front of me with its hazards on.

Celeste rolls down her window and waves at me. I have to admit it. Seeing her drive a nice car like that, especially in a busy city like San Francisco, is hella attractive.

The husky croons of an alternative rock singer greet me when I open the door, along with some percussive beats and futuristic-sounding guitar. Celeste taps her steering wheel to lower the volume and says, "Hey," while I get into the passenger seat.

"Hi."

As I put my bag in the back of the car, I don't miss Celeste's eyes giving me a once-over, and I get a slight satisfactory thrill when her eyes linger on my chest the moment I take off my faux fur coat. I *specifically* wore this blue sundress because of the cleavage it shows off.

"You look beautiful as always," she says, only taking her eyes off me to pull her car back into the flow of traffic.

"You look pretty sexy yourself."

Celeste is impossibly cool in her black leather jacket, heather-gray sweater dress, and white knee-high boots. Along with her blue aviators, she looks like she could star in a car commercial herself instead of being the person who'd shoot one.

"Felt like dressing up," she says, keeping her eyes on the road. "Even if it's mostly a work trip for me."

I shrug. "There's nothing wrong with working in style."

Celeste nods in agreement.

When we reach the coastal part of the road, she presses a button above our heads to open up the moon roof. The salty sea breeze pleasantly chills the inside of the car as we continue our drive up north.

"Sorry," she says. "I should have asked beforehand. Is this too cold for you?"

"No, it's nice. I have my coat."

I've finished putting my coat back on when we reach the Golden Gate Bridge. In the previous times I'd seen the bridge, it'd always been covered, either fully or partially, by the fog. Today, though, the majestic reddish-orange arches are in plain view, taking my breath away.

I take a quick video on my phone as we drive across, and Celeste slows down—or as much as she can in the flow of traffic—so I can fully capture the view.

When we're off the bridge, I tell her, "Thanks."

"No problem," she replies. "Contrary to popular belief, not all professional photographers are condescending assholes who shit on Instagram."

I laugh. "I noticed. Your account has so many followers." The moment I say those words, I want to die of embarrassment. I can't believe I admitted to Celeste that I looked her up on social media. But she's the one whose cheeks turn red.

"You looked up my Instagram?" she asks, uncharacteristically sheepish. "Recently? What did you think?"

"It's great! You have some very cool shots on it. And you have such great range, too. It's no wonder you're such a popular photographer. I got so proud just thinking about how you continued following your passion after college."

"Thanks." Celeste turns away from me and clears her throat. "Anyway. Sorry if this is rude of me, but can you do me a favor while I work?"

"Sure, what's up?"

"Could you please find a good restaurant for us?" she asks. "I ended up having to do a few more things before I picked you up, so I didn't have time to find a place. We can go wherever you want. And again, it's on me."

"Of course! I'll be on my computer anyway, so it's no problem."

A few minutes later, we arrive at a small harbor with picturesque bright white yachts bobbing up and down in the greenish-blue waters.

Two gorgeous—*and very tall*—models, a man and a woman, stand in front of one of the boats. They both wave at us as we get out of Celeste's car. The man is wearing a white tux, like James Bond, while the woman is wearing a red evening gown and Louboutins.

"So clearly I'm not the target demographic for this commercial," I remark as Celeste parks the car.

Celeste grins. "Don't worry. I'm not, either. I'm just here for the job."

When we get out of the car, I take in the beautiful scenery. White mist clings to the mountains behind us, while on the other side of the bay, faraway and faint but still beautiful, is the San Francisco city skyline. Seagulls perch on the waves that brush against the yachts floating on the water. As far as winter in SF goes, it's a nice, relatively sunny day, with the perfect setting to match.

"There's a coffee shop that's a five minutes' walk away from here," Celeste says, taking out her equipment from the back seat. "I double-checked this morning before my errands since I wanted to make sure you had a place to work. Text me if you need anything. And come back around sunset."

"Okay, thanks." I grab my bag from the car.

Celeste gives me a hug before we go our separate ways. It's more than a little chilly, so I linger in her arms a bit more than necessary.

Small trees and quaint storefronts line the way to the coffeehouse, making me feel like I've stepped into another era. The ocean breeze stirs up the skirt of my dress, and I have to hold it in place to avoid a Marilyn Monroe moment.

Fortunately, the coffeehouse is relatively empty, so I'm able to find a nice spot by the window with a beautiful view of the Bay. I order myself a mocha before turning on my computer.

The first order of business, of course, is to find a place to eat dinner, like Celeste requested. As it turns out, there are a lot of great food options in Sausalito, but one in particular catches my attention. Just a few minutes away from the yacht harbor is a fancy pizza place with beautiful nighttime views and a cozy-looking outdoor firepit. The vibes seem immaculate.

The barista calls out my order, and I get my drink before settling back into my seat. I save the restaurant on my phone and move on to my work. Sipping on my mocha, I get done as much as I can, answering emails, drafting a few write-ups, and going through recent submissions to Dear Karl.

When the sun begins to set, coloring the sky a vivid orange and red, I head back to the harbor.

Celeste is alone when I reach her, and as I quietly watch, she snaps a few photos of the horizon with her camera. I stop a few paces away and get out my phone to take a picture of *her*, since she looks especially beautiful in the bright colors of the early evening.

"Hey," Celeste says when she catches sight of me.

"Hey, how'd the shoot go?"

"Not bad." She snaps a few quick more shots, this time of the boats. "The models were great, and the wind was cooperative for once, so everything went smoothly. How about you?"

"I finished the work I couldn't do back at the office."

"Amazing!" Celeste says with a smile. "I'm glad to hear it. Did you have a chance to find where you want to eat?"

"Yup. There's a great pizza place nearby."

"Perfect. Let's go."

By the time we arrive at the unassuming bungalow front of the restaurant, the sun has completely set. The host leads us to the back, and I'm awed by the cozy atmosphere created by the golden yellow string lights hanging above our heads. The patio overlooks a smaller harbor with boats that look adorable and quaint compared to the behemoths Celeste was shooting earlier today. And beyond that is the other side of the bay, lit by bright specks of light from the houses lining the distant hills.

The circular firepit is already occupied by a large, happy family, so Celeste and I sit at one of the tables by the water.

When our waiter arrives, we choose a bottle of wine for the table. After a cursory glance at the menu, Celeste asks me, "Do you want to get the mushroom pizza? Is that still your favorite topping?"

"Yes, it is," I say, blushing. It's amazing how she remembers so many little details about me even after all these years. "But we can get something else, if you want."

"Nah, I like mushrooms, too."

After the waiter comes back and leaves with our order, she stares at me so intensely that I let out a nervous laugh.

"What?" I ask.

"You look gorgeous in this light," she says, getting up from our table. "You're *glowing*. I'll be right back."

Gemma

"No way!" I laugh when Celeste returns with her camera. I cover my face with my hands, suddenly feeling shy.

"Yes way," Celeste says with a gentle smile. "You're beautiful, Gem. And I realized I haven't taken pictures of you with my DSLR yet. Other than for work, I mean." She adjusts the lens of her camera, but then pauses to add, "Do let me know if you're not comfortable with me randomly taking pictures of you, though. It's totally fine."

"I don't mind at all," I reply. "Thank you, Celeste. This is sweet of you."

She takes a few photos of me, some with me looking at the camera, others not. When the waiter brings out our wine, he has an amused grin on his face.

"Would you like me to take a picture of you two, as well?" he asks. "I know a thing or two about cameras."

Celeste hesitates for a split second before she says, "That'd be great. Thank you."

She loops her arm around my shoulders and kisses my cheek, and I laugh as the waiter snaps a photo.

"I don't normally let other people touch my cameras," Celeste whispers to me after he's gone. "But I *really* wanted this picture of us." She reviews the photo and smiles. "And he did a pretty good job. Nice!"

After safely storing the camera back in its case, Celeste pours me a glass of the pinot noir. "For you," she says, handing it to me with a big flourish.

I laugh. "Oh, stop. You're acting like we're on a romantic date or something."

Celeste raises her eyebrows. "I was messing around, but have you gone on a date where someone actually served you wine like *that*? Mr. James Matheson, maybe?"

"Thankfully no," I say, taking a sip of the rich, red wine. "Or else I'd die laughing."

She gives me a teasing smile. "I can see you doing that."

I shrug. "It's not a good idea to try so hard to impress the other person. Dates should be about getting to know each other to see if you have genuine chemistry. Not putting up some front."

If it bothers Celeste that I put my advice columnist cap on, she doesn't show it. She takes a long sip of her wine, growing contemplative. "Fair. So then, I'm curious. What would you say our chemistry is like?"

There she goes again. It's like Celeste can't talk to me for long without flirting.

"Good," I say truthfully. "Natural. I never felt *un*comfortable with you, not even when we first met in college."

Celeste stares at me, biting her red-painted lips before she replies, "Same. Maybe it's because you were a friend of a friend, but I don't think I ever felt awkward with you, either. And I was way more socially anxious back in college, to the point that I could barely get myself to talk to other people. But I always felt like I could talk to you. Well, during the times we were still talking to each other, of course."

I blink. Celeste was always one of the "cool kids" at our school who never seemed to have a shortage of friends around her at any given moment. When we lived together, she'd constantly have guests over at our apartment. To hear that she was socially anxious is a big surprise.

"Oh, I never knew that," I say at last. "You did a good job hiding the anxiety."

Celeste shrugs. "Just because people like me, doesn't necessarily mean I like them back." She laughs. "God, I sound like such an asshole, but I mean that in the least douchey way possible. I'm uncomfortable with most people, because I come from a family where my parents never let me be myself. And, because of the way I look, everyone always assumes I'm a certain way when I'm really not."

I wince, and she laughs at my chagrined expression.

"It's fine," she continues. "Everyone's a little miserably awkward inside, regardless of how popular they are. Especially in college. Some people are just better at hiding it."

"I'll drink to that." I take another sip of my wine.

Celeste does, too. And after she swallows, she says, "With

you . . . I never felt like I needed to be someone else. Living with you was one of the happiest experiences of my life."

I meet her eyes, and her long lashes flutter slightly, as if she's startled by the sudden eye contact. But then her gaze intensifies as it slides down to my lips.

I lean forward and kiss her. Celeste places her wineglass on the table to gently caress my face with her hands. To avoid falling to the ground or causing a spillage, I get off my stool and climb into her lap instead. All I can think about is her dark eyes and how good she feels against my skin.

"I loved living with you, too," I say. "And I feel so comfortable around you, too. I still love—" I bite my lip, catching myself before I can go on.

Celeste's gaze softens, like she knows what I was about to say.

"I love being with you," I finally get out. That's passable, right?

Celeste kisses my forehead. "I love being with you, too."

She moves down to my lips, and we're still making out when the waiter says, "Ahem, pardon me, your pizza is here."

I yelp, causing someone at the firepit to cry out in surprise. I break apart from Celeste, barely managing to avoid knocking over everything. As I resettle into my seat, I keep my eyes on the ground and don't *dare* look up, in case I make eye contact with the family sitting by the fire. God, I completely forgot about them.

Sounding like she's trying very hard not to laugh, Celeste says to the waiter, "Thank you."

"You're welcome."

When the waiter leaves, we both burst into giggles. Suddenly, it's like we're in college all over again.

"Okay, new rule," I say. "No kissing or otherwise touching each other until *after* we get out of here. There are kids present!"

"That's a great idea. I'm sure this food is amazing, but let's eat as fast as we can so we can leave here ASAP."

"Hey, don't rush me! I plan on relishing every single bite."

Celeste sits back in her seat. In a low, sultry voice, she says, "Fine, you can take as much time with the pizza as you want."

"Okay..."

"And then, I promise you, I'll take as much time as *I* want with *you* later in bed."

I swallow. I can't decide whether I like the sound of that or not.

By the time we drive into the garage of our Sausalito Airbnb, I'm so turned on that I hardly notice our surroundings. Getting our stuff from the car and entering the house seems to take a torturously long amount of time, but when Celeste finally locks the door behind us, I don't know what to do in the sudden darkness.

I don't have to wonder for long, though, because Celeste pins me against the wall, knocking the breath out of me.

"Sorry," she says, kissing me along my collarbones before making her way down to the neckline of my dress.

I grab a hold of her hair, clinging to her as she unzips me and captures my right breast with her lips. "Don't apologize. Just don't stop."

My dress drops to the ground, and she steps over it with an amused smile.

"It took so much effort for me to keep my hands off you all day, since I could hardly think of anything else except you in that dress. But I like you so much more without it."

"Oh yeah?" I ask, genuinely surprised. "It didn't seem like you were under that much temptation."

She starts making her way down my stomach, the pleasant sensation of her soft lips on my bare skin making me shudder with pleasure.

"Well," she says in between kisses. "I guess we should be glad you don't read minds for a living. I've been thinking of fucking you all day."

I moan. Just her words are enough to make me even more wet than I already am.

We move to the bed, and I gasp when taking off her clothes reveals an elegant, white lace bodysuit underneath. It beautifully cups her breasts, while the corset part is mesh and has interlacing white floral designs that elegantly contrast with the black flowers on her body. She looks so perfectly sexy and angelic at the same time.

"Were you wearing this underneath your clothes all day?" My core aches at the mere thought.

"I wanted to look good for you," she says, making my heart skip a beat. "Although it did make work a little tricky at times." She chuckles as she sits up. "I also have another surprise in my bag, if you're up for it. No worries at all if you're not comfortable with it, though. Just a sec."

Feeling suddenly underdressed in my plain black underwear, I sit up in the bed while Celeste goes back out into the hallway. My mouth falls open when she returns holding three things: a red bullet vibrator, a black harness, and a hot-pink dildo.

"These are brand-new and clean," she says. "I got them on my way to pick you up."

I swallow. "Am I going to wear that, or are you?"

We'd tried using a variety of toys in college, but Celeste was usually the one to use them on me. At the time, I didn't mind, since I'd always been too intimidated to use anything more than a rabbit vibrator on her. But now...

My lips part, and my heart beats faster at the thought of using the harness with Celeste. I want to try it, especially since I don't know if I'm ever going to be able to use it with her again.

Celeste laughs. "Gem... it's clear from your face that it has to be you. You're practically drooling."

"I mean, I do want to try it, but I have no idea how to even put anything on. It's like how I had no idea how to eat you out."

"Well, you've certainly overcome *that* challenge, so I wouldn't worry too much about this." With a soft smile, Celeste beckons me over. "Come here, Gemma baby. I'll show you."

When I go to her, she helps me fit the dildo into the harness and step through the straps. She then slips the bullet vibrator into the pocket of the harness and helps me make sure everything is secure but not *too* tight around my body before moving away from me.

For a split second, I feel a little awkward with the bright pink strap-on hanging from my crotch. But then Celeste says, “Beautiful. Now turn on the vibrator and get inside me.”

Just her words are enough to turn me on all over again.

I slip my finger inside the pocket and flick on the vibrator, briefly closing my eyes at the soft, pleasant vibrations at my core. I ease into the sensation, steadying my breathing so I can fully stay present.

With a smile, Celeste sits back on the bed. I pull her toward me, starting to kiss her from the flowers on her arms, all the way down to her center folds. By then, I'm shaking, my entire body trembling with each tremor of the vibrator. I can feel my own wetness against my skin as it trickles down from the harness.

But after all she's done for me today, I want Celeste to feel as good as she possibly can. I put all my focus into pleasuring her with my mouth until she's nice and wet for me, alternating between flicking my tongue over her center and sucking her until she's trembling and pulling at my hair.

“Gem,” she gasps. “Gem, please. I want you, desperately.”

I carefully reposition myself so the dildo's head is lined up with her entrance before slowly, gently pushing inside. We both gasp, and I've restrained myself for so long that I almost come right then and there from the sight of the dildo sliding into her. It's a moment straight out of my darkest fantasies, but somehow even better than I could have ever imagined.

"Fuck," I say. "I love being inside you, Celeste."

I begin moving, and her cries echo throughout the room. She claws my back, making me moan as I speed up my thrusts, losing all semblance of control.

I want to keep up the momentum, but since I'm not used to moving like this, especially not for long periods of time, I lose steam. Without missing a beat, Celeste moves away from me and breathlessly says, "Here, sit on the edge of the bed with your legs wide open. Make sure your feet can touch the floor."

I do what she says. With her back turned toward me, she sits in between my legs, gasping with pleasure as she slowly lowers herself onto the dildo.

I bite my lip, somehow even more turned on than I was before.

Pressing herself up against me, Celeste moves up and down in my lap, and I follow her lead, using the bed to help me thrust into her. The best thing about this position, I find out, is that I can also play with her clit. When I start pleasuring her, she cries out, "Don't stop! Just like that!"

We move together, and all I can think is, *Yes, yes, yes.*

"I'm going to come," she says. "I'm so close."

As she continues to ride me, I touch her until she unravels in my arms. Finally, I let go, crying out as white-hot pleasure shoots through me with the incessant waves of the vibrator. We fall back onto the bed, sweaty and panting, but also smiling blissfully at one another while we lie in each other's arms.

"You're a natural," Celeste says.

"I have a good teacher," I reply as I slip off the harness. "Thanks for guiding me through everything."

She gives my forehead a kiss.

I close my eyes for *what I think* is a few seconds, when I wake up to the sound of the faucet running. It eventually stops, and the door to the bathroom opens to reveal Celeste wearing the harness.

I bite my lip. *Holy crap.*

A devilish grin playing on her lips, she comes to stand by the bed, smelling like water and jasmine-scented soap.

I have a very good idea about what's going to happen next. But I still ask, "What are you doing?"

Celeste reaches out to take my chin in her hand. "Oh, Gemma baby," she says slowly in a voice that's so sexy my breath catches. "Who said we were done? Remember what I said back at the restaurant?"

I'm still smiling sheepishly when Celeste roughly grabs my hair.

"Get on your knees," she commands in a way that makes my legs go weak.

Oh, dear God.

And Celeste shows me just how well she keeps her promises.

Celeste

Celeste and Gemma are still crossing the Golden Gate Bridge when Gemma's phone rings. She lets the call go to voicemail and puts the phone to her ear to listen to the message. Her voice pitching higher with panic, she says, "It's Rob. He and Marge are already at the studio!"

Celeste lets out a frustrated groan as she presses on the gas. "We still have a full hour left! Why are they so early?"

She's lightheaded from the fact that she and Gemma got barely any sleep the previous night, but thankfully, she can still drive. The only thing that's keeping her going right now is the thought of her coffeepot patiently waiting for her at the studio.

"I'll send him a text saying they can wait at the café next door." Gemma taps away at her phone.

"Thanks."

The one plus side of the morning's chaos is that it doesn't

give her and Gemma the chance to talk about things. Their picture-perfect mini vacation to Sausalito—and this entire week, really—had been way better than Celeste expected, filled with not just a lot of good sex but a lot of heart-to-hearts, too. Celeste doesn't know what to do with herself, nor the undeniable feelings she has for Gemma.

When they arrive at the studio, Rob is predictably grouchy, but he's no match for Celeste. Especially not now. To distract herself from her own messy and confusing swirl of emotions, Celeste puts her charm into full gear. By the time she's done setting up, she, Rob, and Marge are all chatting and laughing like she's their long-lost granddaughter.

Rob is approaching eighty-five, while Marge is "young," according to her husband, at almost eighty. As Celeste finishes her coffee, the couple says they've been married for *sixty* years, more than two times her age.

Gemma begins the interview, Celeste quietly walks around, slowly circling the space with her camera like she usually does. Rob and Marge are both white. Their faces are wrinkled, and their backs are stooped with age. Rob is bald, with thick gray eyebrows that Celeste can tell used to be black, while Marge has white, curly hair that used to be golden.

Celeste never knew her grandparents, since the ones on her dad's side opposed her parents' marriage and never bothered to be a part of her life, while her mom's parents passed before she could form any real memories of them. The only thing Celeste remembers is what her mom told her when she was little.

"Your grandparents loved each other very much to their dying day," she'd say. "It's the reason why I've always believed in love."

As Celeste takes pictures of the couple's joined hands and the little knowing smiles that they occasionally give each other, Celeste wonders if this is what her grandparents were like, too. She grins at the thought.

Celeste usually only half listens to what Gemma and the interviewees say, since she's too busy figuring out the best shots or checking on the cameras. So she misses the first part of the conversation, but she does catch Rob say, "When I was in my seventies, I felt like I could do anything. Past eighty though? Forget about it. Take me to the nearest crematorium."

Celeste covers her mouth before her laughter can burst through and ruin the recording. As the interview progresses, she notices that Gemma adds a couple more questions than usual, like, "Has your opinion of each other changed from when you got married to now?"

"Of course!" Rob says. "I love her even more now than I did back then." At the same time Marge replies, "No, not really. I always loved him a lot, then and now."

Celeste's favorite moment is when Gemma asks the couple about their future plans.

With a completely deadpan face, Rob says, "Die."

Even Celeste can't help but snicker this time. She'll have to edit the sound out later.

Gemma wraps up like she always does, by asking, "How would you define love?"

"Love is hard work," Rob starts to say, before Marge adds, "It's going through decades together and somehow not hating each other. Or at least, tolerating each other enough that you can still live under the same roof."

Both Rob and Gemma burst out laughing.

"Fifty percent of American couples don't make it this far." Rob makes the sign of the cross. "Lord have mercy. Did we get lucky! Whatever happened to 'till death do us part'?"

He looks at the ceiling as if asking the question to God himself.

"It's because women don't have to keep being married to men they don't like anymore, you big doofus," Marge says. "We can make money now. And escape if we want to."

"Well!" Rob exclaims loudly, making Celeste startle. "Then I guess I better treat you twice as good as I already do so you won't run away from me!"

Marge smiles. "Oh, hush, you already treat me plenty well enough."

~

When the final couple for "Modern Love in Focus," Keiko and Nat, enters the studio, Celeste freezes. Her eyes remain fixed on Keiko, and in that moment, it occurs to Celeste that she's never seen a queer Asian elder before, and definitely not one who is sapphic like her. Most of the other queer people she knows are around her age or younger, and the few older individuals she knows are not Asian. It's a realization that sends her reeling, reminding her of a conversation she had with Min-joon while he was visiting over the holidays.

After hanging out with her friends in LA, they'd gone back to her place to have some barbecued pork belly and a bottle of soju. A few shots in, he'd randomly said, "You know, I've never heard anyone say they have a gay *harabeoji* or even a gay *samchon*. Have you?"

"No," Celeste had replied. "You just never hear that sort of thing in Korea."

Unlike her LA friends, who openly talked about their queer relatives, Min-joon and her other friends back home never mentioned having a gay grandpa or even a gay uncle, or any queer relatives at all.

"It's the culture difference," Min-joon had said. "It's not like Korean queers don't exist. *We* exist. But a lot of people remain closeted and live with the wife or husband they hate, more so than they do here. Let's *not* do that."

In the present, Celeste's hands slightly tremble as she gets Keiko and Nat set up. She takes a few pictures of them before she begins the recording, making sure to capture every detail. The matching laugh lines on Keiko's and Nat's faces. Keiko's wrinkly, golden hands resting on Nat's dark brown ones.

When they begin the interview, the couple talks about how they met in the seventies while Nat was an exchange student in Tokyo.

"By the end of the program, I managed to convince her to move to America with me," Nat says with a laugh.

"It didn't seem so scary at the time," Keiko adds with a laugh of her own. "Since on the map, it was 'just' an ocean away. How brave I was back then!"

"Mind you, San Francisco in the seventies was not the same city it is now," Nat continues. "The civil rights movement had just happened ten years ago. But SF still seemed like a better place for us to live together at the time, especially after the Pride parades, newspapers, and rights ordinances started popping up."

"Meanwhile in Japan," Keiko says. "My parents were very upset when they found out about Nat. Even today, same-sex marriage is not allowed there like it is here, but I am hoping it'll happen soon."

Celeste tightens her grip on the camera, thinking of her own parents and how Korea has also yet to legalize same-sex marriage.

"We'd already been together for about forty years when we got legally married here, in SF," Nat says with a laugh. "But it was nice to finally have that slip of paper. Our kids got a real kick out of it, since they got marriage certificates of their own around the same time."

She and Keiko share a smile, and Celeste captures the moment with her camera.

When Gemma asks about their biggest challenges, Keiko answers, "Living far away from home was always the most difficult thing for me. My parents, my brothers, and my cousins... they all eventually accepted my relationship with Nat. But by then, I already had a life that I didn't want to leave here. I don't regret my choices, but I wish I could have spent more time with my family while they were still alive."

Tears fall from Keiko's eyes, and Celeste thinks about the last several years of her own life. She can somewhat relate to Keiko, since, after a childhood of constantly being told something was wrong with her, she'd thought she could just never look back after moving to the US. But she still gets a pang of homesickness whenever she leaves Korea and lands back in LAX. She misses her family and wishes she could see Min-joon and the rest of her friends in Seoul more often.

In an ideal world, she could live the life she wants *and* be accepted by her family back home. But of course, that world doesn't exist, and it probably won't for a long time.

Her eyes glistening in the light, Nat squeezes Keiko's hand. "She gave up so much to be here with me. And I'm grateful for it, every day."

"That's so sweet," Gemma says. She wipes her tears away before asking the next question. "Have there been any changes within your relationship throughout the years?"

"Our lives are definitely different now," Nat replies. "I mean, we have *grandkids*. It still blows my mind whenever I think about it. But our relationship, itself? Not really."

Keiko nods. "We've both changed plenty throughout the decades, and we keep experiencing new things every year. But our love has remained constant, the anchor that has gotten us through all of life's challenges."

Nat nods. "Couldn't have said it better myself."

Is that why Celeste has felt so unmoored all her life, going from parents who never fully accepted her to countless different lovers, some of whose faces and names she's already forgotten? Her vision blurs, and she slowly exhales.

Finally, Gemma asks the question she's asked every couple, the final question of this entire project. "How do you define love?"

Celeste braces herself.

"Breathing," Keiko says, looking into Nat's eyes.

"Living," Nat replies. "I can't imagine life without my wife."

Keiko and Nat stare lovingly at each other, and Celeste can't take it anymore. She sets her camera down on the table beside her.

Gemma shoots her a concerned look. "Celeste?" she says. "Are you okay?"

Unable to verbalize the whirlwind of thoughts and feelings inside her head, Celeste meets Gemma's gaze and backs away.

For the first time in years, the future she wants for herself is so clear. So obvious, to the point of being right in front of her very eyes.

She wants to spend the rest of her life with Gemma. She wants to marry her and have kids with her and grow old with her, laughing and crying together for decades on end like the two women sitting on the couch. Even the slightest possibility of not being able to have that future becomes an unbearable weight.

"Sorry," she says to no one and to everyone. "I have to go."

Then, before anyone can stop her, Celeste bolts out of the studio.

35

Gemma

After apologizing and saying goodbye to a startled and confused Keiko and Nat, I set off to find Celeste. It takes me a while, but I eventually find her in the restroom of a nearby bar, thanks to a server who saw her run full speed past him.

At first, I'm confused as to why Celeste ran in *here* out of all places. But then, over the deafeningly loud music being blasted from the speakers, I hear the faintest sob.

My chest aches. She must have come here in the hopes that the music would drown out the sound of her crying.

"Celeste?" I say, practically yelling to be heard over the screaming guitars.

I knock on the stall door as gently as I can.

The crying stops. Seconds pass. I'm afraid Celeste is going to leave me out here, awkwardly standing in the middle of the restroom, when there's a barely audible click.

Celeste slowly opens the door, rendering me speechless. Her usually perfect makeup is smeared all over, with eyeliner and mascara running down her face.

I've never seen her like this, not even while we were together in college.

"Nat and Keiko left," I tell her, still speaking at twice my normal volume. "So we have the studio to ourselves again. Do you want to go back there to talk about things? It's too loud here!"

Celeste nods. I wrap my arm around her shoulders as we exit the bar.

Back in the studio, we sit down on the couch where Keiko and Nat were moments before. But now, the cameras are off, and it's just Celeste and me, face-to-face, off the record.

I place a hand on Celeste's in what I hope is a comforting gesture. "What's wrong?" I ask, as gently as I can.

Celeste takes a deep breath. "What Keiko said about her family... it dug up a lot of unpleasant memories for me. My family is similar. I don't know if I told you, but when I was back in Korea, my mom and her relatives pressured me to date guys. This was after I found out you'd moved on, and I was toying with the idea that I could be bisexual like you and Min-joon. So I tried it. But nope. It was horrible."

I scrunch up my nose. "Ugh, I'm so sorry. Hearing Keiko talk about her experiences must have been triggering for you."

Celeste cocks her head to the side in acknowledgment. "Kind of. But also, seeing Nat and Keiko like that, living their happily-ever-afters despite everything life threw at them. For fifty years!"

She starts crying again, not full-on sobbing like before, but silent tears that trickle down her cheeks. Almost instinctively, I wrap my arms around her and kiss away the droplets. She leans forward, slowly making her way to my lips. Unlike the other times we've made out, today we're slower, but more passionate. Gentle, but more intense.

When we stop to breathe, Celeste kisses me on the forehead. "Gemma, you're always so good to me," she says with a small grin. "Thank you for trying to cheer me up."

I frown. Her words are innocuous, and in any other context, I would have smiled and said, "Sure." But here, at this very moment, my heart drops. I'm not here, sitting on the couch with my arms wrapped around Celeste as she cries, just to try to "cheer her up." I'm here because of something far more than that. Because I *want* something more than that. Before I can stop myself, I blurt out, "Celeste... what you said about Nat and Keiko... what's to say that we can't have that? Why can't that be us, too?"

She stiffens, the smile freezing on her lips.

My shoulders drop, but I forge on. "I know you're scared that we won't work out. And I know it seems like we can't have what they have, that we can't have a happy ending of our own, especially because of our past. But it's been *eight years* since all that shit happened. You're here now, older and wiser, and so am I. Isn't that all that matters? Why can't we try again?"

Celeste stares at me like I've sprouted another head.

"Gem," she says quietly. "I thought we agreed to keep things casual."

Frustration builds up inside me as I gesture at her and me. "Does any of this feel casual to you?" I ask, my voice coming out louder than I intended. "Because, in retrospect, none of what we did together in the past month or so feels that casual to me, regardless of what we called it."

She closes her eyes briefly, wincing as if in real physical pain. Her voice is low and flat as she replies, "You told me yourself... *less than two weeks ago*, that you're not looking to seriously date anyone right now. Didn't your *engagement* end in November? And you were with him for, what, seven years?"

"Well, yeah, but he moved on quickly, too. And—"

"If it takes you *two months* to move on from someone you were *engaged to*... wow, it must have taken you a week to get over me."

I flinch, like she's slapped me across the face. But the sting of her words is worse than any physical pain I've ever experienced. "It was a few months, and I already apologized to you for that."

But Celeste is relentless. She pulls away from me and sits with her legs folded against her chest. "When's the last time you've been single, Gem?" she asks, staring right into my eyes. "*Really.*"

I open my mouth to answer her. But my thoughts grind to a halt. I realize I can't remember the last time I was completely single. Before I even met Celeste, I went out with a few guys from school here and there. And after her, well...

When I'm unable to say anything, she sighs. Unfolding her legs so her feet are on the ground again, she finally turns away from me.

"I'm not like you, Gem," she says softly. "I love that you love people so much. I love how you can fall in love so easily and trust others again. You always see the best in people, and that's amazing. It's one of my favorite things about you. But that's not *me*. While you moved on and got engaged, and Kayla got married and even had kids... I couldn't do any of that."

She laughs, but her voice sounds so broken and pained that it brings tears to my eyes. "Even though I'm glad we cleared the air about the past, I'm still so fucking scared. I don't want to enter into something serious with you when I know I'm not ready. And nothing you've said has given me the confidence I need to trust that you won't tell me you want to spend your entire life with me and then just change your mind a few months later again."

"Celeste, I—" I try to go on, to tell Celeste that this time will be different because we won't randomly break up again like we did when we were a couple of college kids. We're older now. And we know better. But the truth is, I have no way of guaranteeing that. And it's so clear to me now that we're *definitely* not ready for what I want. What *we* want.

She caresses my face and wipes my tears away with her thumbs. "I love you, Gem. I really do. I can't even begin to express in words how much I care about you. Earlier, I completely lost it because it hit me how much I want to grow old with you. How much I want us to have what Nat and Keiko have. But if we fuck up again, it'll absolutely *kill* me."

She's full-on sobbing again. And this time, so am I. "I love you, too."

Celeste wraps her arms around me, and I squeeze her tight. Although neither of us say anything, I get the feeling this is the last time I'll be able to hug her for a while.

We stay like that for a long moment before she pulls away from me, wiping the rest of her tears away.

"Okay," she says softly, squeezing my hand. "I'll give you a ride back to your friends' place."

After Celeste drops me off at the apartment, I crawl onto Clementine. Burrito jumps up and meows before settling next to me. His warmth is comforting, and I wrap myself around him as tightly as I can without squishing him. Luckily, he's always been a cuddly cat.

My friends must be out doing something in the city, because they're nowhere to be seen. It is Saturday night after all.

A few hours later, Celeste sends me all the files from today, without a subject or a message as usual. I don't know why I expected anything different from her, but my heart still sinks when my phone stays dark the rest of the night.

Before I go to sleep, I write a formal apology to Nat and Keiko for their interview's abrupt end. Without going into personal details, I thank them for their time and tell them that both Celeste and I were very deeply moved by what they told us. Since I don't think she'll mind, I cc Celeste and send the email before focusing on wrapping up the project.

We're somehow already five weeks away from Valentine's Day, making us a bit behind schedule. But since work is a good distraction from everything else, I end up being super productive and make up for lost time.

By Monday morning, I've finished the write-up, added Celeste's pictures, and sent everything to Evelyn for review.

I'm sad, but not surprised, when I don't hear from Celeste again.

Gemma

I don't have the heart—or strength—to tell my friends what happened yet. But even without me saying anything, Val and Kiara seem to sense that something is wrong, because they give me extra-long hugs when I move out later that week.

"You're always welcome back anytime," Kiara tells me after she and Val help me move my box to Ms. Chang's apartment.

"Burrito will miss you," Val says. "We will, too, of course. But we'll still see each other at work every day."

I pout. "Aw, I'll miss Burrito, too! He's the best. I'll definitely come over to visit him!"

I'm glad I had the foresight to schedule my move-in day when I did, because it turns out to be perfect distraction from everything that happened with Celeste. For the next two weeks, I have my hands full with making the room into my new home. It's not as spacious as the condo I lived in with James, but after living several months on my friends' couch, just having my own bed feels like a huge luxury.

My new landlady, Ms. Chang, and her husband, Mr. Lieu, are a nice, older Asian couple who are recent empty nesters. Ms. Chang, I learn, frequently cooks when she's nervous, so the apartment always smells of delicious food whether she's at home or not. She also sometimes even makes me snacks and meals like she were my own mom, waving me away and saying they had extra when I tell her she doesn't have to give me any.

In return, I try to help Ms. Chang and her husband by quelling their anxieties about their kid, who just started as a spring admit at USC. Funnily enough, I went to their *rival* school. But whenever we sit down together for dinner, I answer whatever questions the nervous parents—or sometimes their daughter herself through WeChat—have about college and living in LA, in general. It's the kind of serendipitous and comforting connection with strangers that I didn't know I needed until now.

Meanwhile at work, after a few more rounds of revisions with Evelyn, our project gets finalized as *Horizon*'s cover story for February. I want to share the good news with Celeste, but I don't, respecting her decision to go silent on me. I'm sure she'll find out about it, sooner or later.

All in all, it really does seem like I left last year's bad energy behind, because everything in my life goes smoothly for once. The only times I don't feel okay are at night, in the quiet hours when I'm alone in my bed and acutely aware of my every breath.

In these dark moments, every single thought threatens to swallow me whole, like a thick, suffocating blanket. I wonder if I'll ever stop missing Celeste, if I'll ever be okay with being by myself.

Upon its release on Valentine's Day, the online version of "Modern Love in Focus," along with the corresponding interview videos, gets a record number of clicks. Print sales also skyrocket, with countless people buying the printed issue as a keepsake, thanks to Celeste's gorgeous photos.

People tag Celeste and me on Instagram, making posts and stories about how they could relate to different interviews. I try to reshare every story I see, and when I see Celeste's icon appear under the list of people who've seen my stories, I feel a sense of comfort knowing that, on some level, she's still there, even while she's keeping her distance.

The most popular interview so far is Brent and Aaron's, which is to be expected because of Brent's massive social media following. But Keiko and Nat's also makes the rounds, with many other queer women posting excerpts from their interview.

I've literally never seen an older sapphic couple interviewed like this before, someone says in the comments. This is such important representation in a day

and age when the portrayal of queer elders, especially people of color, is so rare!

A few other people on social media mention they've followed Dear Karl for a while, sending heart emojis our way and recalling specific instances the other writers and I have helped them over the years. All in all, most of the feedback seems to be positive.

"Well done," Evelyn says after inviting me to her office one morning. "We got great feedback from Citrine. They've decided to keep the lifestyle section and make 'Modern Love in Focus' an annual Valentine's Day tradition, but with different couples each year."

"Oh wow," I say. "That's fantastic!"

Even though it's technically good news, the most I can give her is a tight grin, since it's unlikely that either Celeste or I will want to do this project again. Not after what happened the first time.

Evelyn surprises me by also remaining pensive. I didn't tell her what happened between Celeste and me, so it's not like she could have any idea about any of the non-work stuff. But then why this muted, thoughtful response?

"What is it?" I ask, fearing the worst.

"I saw a job posting," she finally says.

I hold my breath, hoping she's not about to say she's leaving me and the rest of our team. After seven years of working for her, Evelyn *is Horizon* to me. I can't imagine being here at this company without her.

"For a features editor in the New York magazine owned by Citrine," Evelyn continues. "I want you to apply."

I do a double take. "Wait, what? Me?"

"Yes, you, Gemma," Evelyn says with a scoff. "Believe me, I'm far too old for that job. I was looking up retirement homes in San Diego this morning."

"You're retiring?" Panic fills my heart once more at the thought of her leaving.

She waves me off. "In the near future, yes, but you're missing the point, Gemma dear! Honestly, we should have given you a promotion years ago, but we simply couldn't afford it because of all the revenue issues we have at this office. But the New York one, however…"

"They have more money," I say.

"And more opportunities for advancement. In any case, think about it. And if you're interested in applying for that position, I'll be more than happy to give them my recommendation."

My heart races. On one hand, this new job sounds like a dream come true. And especially after everything that happened to me in San Francisco in the last year or so, I feel ready to move to a new place. But at the same time, a part of me wonders if everything will be *too* new. I'm not twenty-two anymore. I'm turning thirty in less than a month.

And like SF, NYC isn't cheap. But at least I'm familiar with San Francisco, and California in general, while I've never even been to the East Coast. Everything I've ever known has been in the West Coast, from my family to my friends.

"Thank you," I say at last. "I'll think about it."

Gemma

In the end, I decide not to apply for the position, a choice that's cemented in my mind when, in the beginning of March, my friends rent out a whole karaoke cable car for my thirtieth birthday.

Although cable cars are relatively common in the city, I almost never ride them. I last took one when I first slept over at Celeste's place in Nob Hill. And before that, the only other time was when James and I rode in the back of the Powell Street trolley to Fisherman's Wharf, hugging each other as the bright red cable car sped down the hills.

Tonight, my friends and I get on what is more of a motorized trolley on wheels. So it's technically not an actual cable car, *but* it more than makes up for the discrepancy with its built-in open bar and karaoke system.

"We thought it'd be a shame if we let this milestone birthday pass without doing something super fun," Kiara says as we settle into our seats. "Plus, your birthday is on a Friday this year, so obviously, we had to go all out!"

"Happy birthday, Gemma!" Val exclaims as the car starts moving.

Kiara joins in, and we all tightly hug each other.

"Thanks, guys," I say. "This is amazing. Literally the best birthday present ever."

We say cheers and down our first round of drinks.

As the car rolls through the streets, we raise our drinks and belt out Chappell Roan songs, as well as hits that were popular while we were in college, like Taylor Swift's "Blank Space" and Adele's "Hello." My friends thankfully don't judge me when I cry through most of the songs, although they do exchange concerned glances when I sing "Casual" a bit too passionately.

When the last notes fade away, Val pauses the music before it can start our next round of songs.

"So," she says. "Do you want to talk about it?"

She doesn't need to clarify what "it" is.

"It's obvious, isn't it?" I say with a laugh that sounds sad and pathetic even to my own ears. "I caught feelings. But in my defense, I'm pretty sure Celeste did, too. I doubt things were casual for her, either. She told me she loves me."

Val winces, and Kiara frowns.

"But then why isn't she here with you?" Val asks. "If she loves you, too, I mean."

I sigh and down my flute of champagne. "She was too afraid to try again, given our history. And honestly, I don't blame her. She went through a lot in the past eight years. A lot more than I did. Also, when she asked me when was the last time I was *single* single for an extended amount of time, I couldn't give her an answer. Even *I* was spooked by that."

Val crosses her arms over her chest in a contemplative gesture. "Oh, yeah. I can't remember a time when you were completely single, either. Very briefly after you split up from James, maybe. But even that didn't last long. And James wasn't your first boyfriend, right? Even though Celeste was your first girlfriend."

I nod. "I dated a few more guys before I met her, when I still thought I was straight."

Kiara pats me on the back. "Then maybe it's good you're taking a break from dating!" With a guilty look, she adds, "Sorry for pushing you to start dating again so soon after your breakup with James. I thought it would help."

"Yeah, I'm sorry, too," Val adds. "For whatever part I played in this."

I shake my head. "It's not either of your faults. This is a personal issue of mine that's been going on way before I even met you guys. I just never realized it until now. I signed up for therapy this week. In the spirit of turning thirty."

Val lifts her glass up. "Hey, good for you! Take charge of that mental health."

Kiara and I giggle at Val's dad energy.

"In all seriousness," Kiara says. "I'm so proud of you, Gemma. We both are. Yay for working on ourselves in this new decade!"

We throw back our drinks, and I clear my throat. "Anyway, thanks, but enough about me. Sorry, I feel like it's been nothing but me-me-me since my breakup with James. How is everything going for you guys?"

Kiara shakes her head. "You were going through a lot, Gem. Seven years is a long time. And then all that stuff with Celeste?" She lets out a baffled laugh. "We're glad we could be there for you. I know you'd do the same if anything happened to us."

Val's eyebrows shoot up in panic. "*Dios mío*, please, let's not even think about that remote possibility. Especially not after—"

She cuts herself off. Her eyes widen as she shoots a glance at Kiara, who also suddenly looks frantic. Kiara mouths something to her girlfriend that suspiciously looks a lot like *Not the right time!*

I then realize that neither Val nor Kiara gave me a real answer when I asked them what they've been up to. I look from one friend to the other. With a nervous laugh, I say, "You can tell me, whatever it is. What's up?"

Val sighs. Then without saying another word, she raises her left hand, and so does Kiara. Kiara has rings on almost all her fingers, so it's not immediately obvious with her, but it definitely is with Val, who never wears any jewelry whatsoever. Except today. And I guess, now, for the rest of her life.

Around each of their left ring fingers is a thin black band. Kiara's has a small, yellow-green stone in the center that I'm pretty sure is peridot, Val's birthstone, while Val's has a ruby—Kiara's birthstone—in the same place. Their engagement rings are both so uniquely them that tears immediately spring to my eyes.

"Oh my gosh," I say. "Finally! Congratulations! Also, wow, I can't believe I'm only noticing them now. They're gorgeous!"

Val gives me a sneaky grin. "Luckily I'm right-handed, so I've been keeping my left hand in my pocket around you for the last couple of days."

I laugh as my brain plays back the last few times I've seen Val this week at lunch. She's right. I only remember her using her right hand.

"Wait, that's so funny!" I exclaim. "But also, you guys didn't have to hide this from me. I'm so, so happy for you two!"

Val shrugs. "We didn't want to be insensitive. Especially after everything you went through last year."

"And it's *your* birthday, Gemma," Kiara adds. "Really, this could have waited at least another day."

I shake my head rapidly. "No, I don't mind at all. If anything, this has made my thirtieth all the more special. My two favorite people in the whole world, getting married! Tell me everything. How did you guys propose? *Who* proposed? Are there pictures?"

Val launches into the story of how she proposed a couple of nights ago—"during the full moon, the culmination of our relationship," Kiara adds with a content sigh—on the rooftop patio of their apartment building.

"I had to hound our landlord until he let me light candles and spread rose petals up there," Val says. "But thankfully he eventually allowed it after I promised I wouldn't tell the other tenants. I also cleaned up everything right away, so no issues there."

She shows me absolutely gorgeous pictures of the dreamy, flowery rooftop proposal, along with stunning snapshots of her and Val kissing under the full moon. There's even an adorable photo of Burrito wearing a little cat tux.

I'm full-on bawling now, my heart bursting with so much joy. Val and Kiara get sniffly, too, and soon, we're all crying and laughing as we hug each other.

"I love you guys *so* much, but also..." I say, pulling away to give Val a side-eye. "Did you not need help with the proposal? I was free that day."

Val shakes her head. "Nah, I was super nervous, so I didn't tell *anyone* except the photographer I hired. And the landlord, of course. But only because I had to. We *could* use your help with something else, though!"

She exchanges glances with Kiara, who nods and takes my hand.

"Gemma, will you be my maid of honor? *Our* maid of honor?"

Both she and Val give me a wide, hopeful smile.

"Of course I will!" I shriek, before pulling my friends into another big hug.

After we wipe away our tears, the three of us launch into Beyoncé's "Cuff It," one of Kiara's favorite songs. We also do "Single Ladies," of course, with my friends hyping me up whenever Beyoncé sings "single ladies" and waving their left hands in the air at "put a ring on it."

At the end of the song, Val pulls Kiara into a sweeping, deep kiss, and I pop open another bottle of champagne.

When I was in college, I thought that by the time I turned thirty, I'd be living in the suburbs with my partner and kids. Drunkenly singing along to Chappell Roan and Beyoncé with my friends in a neon-light-decked trolley car speeding down the hills in San Francisco is like the exact opposite of that. But I'm so fucking happy, I don't care.

My life isn't what I thought it would be. But I'm loving it, regardless.

By the time we get off the car, the three of us are laughing and swaying on the sidewalk, with Val still humming the last couple of songs. It's the most fun I've had in years.

Later that night, I get into my bed at Ms. Chang's and check my phone, like I always do before going to sleep. A single unread notification waits for me on the screen, and I swipe it to reveal a text from Celeste.

Happy birthday, Gem.

A warm rush of emotions fills my chest, along with a sharp pang of bittersweet. After trying and failing to decide how to reply to her, I heart the message and hug my pillow tightly to my chest before drifting off to sleep.

Gemma

The next Monday, James, of all people, approaches my desk.

"Hey, hope you had a good birthday," he says.

Regretting my decision to work through lunch, I keep my attention focused on my computer and my tuna sandwich, determined not to say a word to him.

"I was wondering," he goes on, undeterred by my lack of a reaction. "Can I talk to you in private? Not now, obviously. But after work."

I frown at just the thought of having a one-on-one conversation with him.

And then he asks me the question that makes my stomach recoil.

"Do you want to come over for some drinks? For old times' sake."

I stare at him with an open mouth. *How does James even*

have the nerve to invite me for drinks at the condo that used to be our *home?*

He chuckles nervously. "Look, I still have all the stuff you left in the closet. And I know it's been several months, but I…I feel like I never explained to you why we…you know. Maybe we can talk while you come get your stuff? Sorry it took so long to get to this point. I think I needed some time to process."

But then, I finally hear it. The sadness in his voice. The wretched grief and pain that I wanted to hear from him since that first Monday I saw him after the breakup.

I frown. "Did you and Daphne break up?"

He sighs, running a hand through his hair. "Yeah. But that's not why I came to talk to you, I swear. Or at least, I don't want to get back together or anything. Breaking up with Daphne made me realize how fucked up our breakup left me. And I figured, you probably understand that more than anyone."

I think back to all the things *I* did after our breakup and wince. Plus, I never found out why James decided to end our engagement. Closure, I guess, would be nice.

I also want my stuff back, now that I have the space for everything.

"Okay," I finally say.

Later today, we leave the office together, and I notice small changes in the late afternoon light. James's hair is longer and shaggier than he usually cut it when we were dating. His glasses are different, too, gray instead of the black frames he had when we were together. He seems a lot older, more mature somehow, although realistically he probably doesn't have more than one or two new wrinkles. I wonder if our breakup aged me as well.

He's familiar and foreign, all at once.

We walk mostly in silence to our—*his*—condo, only talking occasionally when he brings up the new food trucks or stores that popped up since the last time we walked this path together. He also asks about me and my parents, and I ask him about his family. I hate to admit it, but catching up like this is nice. After all, we dated for seven years, and it's not like we hated each other's loved ones during the time we were together.

I guess there will always be a part of my life that's enmeshed with him, like a part of his will always be with me.

When we get to the condo, James says, "So, I've made quite a few changes since, um... you moved out."

He opens the door, and my jaw drops open. When we lived together, our condo wasn't exactly spacious, but it was very cozy and warm, with shelves full of books and plants. We also had a TV, on which James and I binge-watched shows and played video games together, all while our soft, plush rug kept our feet warm.

Now, the TV's still there, but everything else is gone, replaced by sleek leather sofas and a black coffee table. There's not even a hint that I used to live here, and I don't know if I feel sad or amazed. If I didn't recognize the floor plan, I'd wonder if this is even the same condo.

"Looks like a real bachelor pad," I say flatly. "You did a good job redecorating the place."

"Thanks," he replies. "It took me a while to figure out what I was doing, but I think I'm finally getting somewhere. All the home and real estate articles I wrote for *Horizon* finally came in handy."

What are you doing? a voice says in the back of my head. *Get out of here. This isn't your home anymore.*

James opens the closet door to reveal four boxes stacked together. I can only assume that's all my stuff. James carries them to the living room, and I sit on one of the sofas to go through and make sure I have everything.

Before I can even process what he's doing, James goes to the kitchen and comes back with two glasses and an all-too-familiar bottle.

My stomach turns. "Isn't that the wine we bought the last time we went to Napa with your parents?" I wince, thinking about the post I had to delete from my Instagram.

A pained look also flashes across James's face. "I know. I couldn't bring myself to drink it after..." He trails off and clears his throat, before trying again. "What better time to drink it than now, right?"

I smile tightly and accept a glass of wine from James. But I don't make any real move to drink it. And neither does he.

"So..." James settles down on the couch beside me with his own glass in one hand. Thankfully, he maintains a careful distance, probably to avoid making things even weirder. Compared to how close we sat together in this living room in the past, the way we're sitting now feels strange, like we've fallen into some kind of parallel universe.

"So?" I set my wine down on the coffee table.

"Are you..." He laughs awkwardly and continues, "Still with that girl? Celeste, right? Your college ex. I was surprised to see her at the New Year's party. I thought she moved to Korea, or at least, that's what I remember you telling me."

"No," I reply. I don't elaborate.

"Oh, okay. Daphne and I were seeing each other, but it was...a bit of a roller coaster. I learned the hard way that I'm not ready for another relationship."

My ears perk up with surprise, but I pretend not to be interested. Instead, I keep my eyes focused on my hands and say, "And you're telling me this why?"

James shrugs. "I thought you'd want to know."

I don't respond. James has dated me long enough to know all my tells, so he correctly interprets my silence as curiosity.

"I regret it, you know," he continues, his normally loud and confident voice coming out so quietly that it gives me pause. For once, he almost sounds *vulnerable*. "Breaking up with you, I mean. I was...scared. After we got engaged, everything got so serious. Marriage, kids, all of that was suddenly around the corner, like boom, boom, boom. I missed the days when we could have fun without thinking about all that serious stuff."

"*You* proposed to me, James," I reply. "*You* decided to take the next step with me."

"I know. But also, like, of course I did! The one thing I was sure about was my feelings about you. Everything else, though..." He sighs. "In retrospect, I wish I hadn't called things off when I did."

A thrill of satisfaction runs through me. But I keep my voice low and steady when I ask, "Then why did you?"

The day we broke up, I walked away from this condo without getting a straight answer from him. I just *let* that slide, allowing James to tear my life apart without even knowing why. Granted, if I'm being fair to myself, I was in a lot of shock and pain. But today, I'm completely calm. Keeping my eyes fixed on his, I cross my arms across my chest and wait.

James sighs again, and nervously says, "Look, this isn't how I wanted this conversation to go. I mean, come on, you're thirty now, too, so you know what it's like...it's terrifying..."

He can't even meet my gaze. In fact, he's staring down at the floor, doing everything in his power to *not* make eye contact with me. I'm hit with the memory of how he acted the Monday after the breakup. Like I was invisible. Before, I thought it was some superiority complex, an arrogant display of "I'm perfectly fine without you." But now, in my much calmer state, I realize he's not trying so hard to avoid eye contact because he thinks he's better than me.

He's avoiding it because he's *hiding something.*

I'm suddenly reminded of how Daphne glared at me in the printer room a couple weeks after James's and my breakup. How, unlike James, she didn't even try to talk to me at the holiday party. She didn't act like she was embarrassed or ashamed to be someone's fast, messy rebound. She treated me like *I* was an interloper. In *their* relationship.

"Did you sleep with Daphne?" I ask. "While we were still together. Is that why you wanted to break up?"

James's eyes widen. But he doesn't say anything, keeping his gaze fixed on the floor.

That's all the answer I need.

Anger rolls and crackles through my chest. I get to my feet and explode, like I did the day he broke up with me. "You know what, James, first of all, fuck you." My voice comes out strained with pain and disbelief. "Really, how *dare* you get engaged to me and then just…cheat like I meant nothing to you? If you were that unsatisfied in our relationship, why couldn't you tell me without wasting seven years of my life?"

James gets on his feet, too. He finally meets my gaze, and I'm taken aback by how there's not even a single bit of remorse in his face. He looks *angry*.

"Because I still loved you!" he yells. "I was just…*scared.* I only started seeing Daphne as a way to blow off steam so I could stay with *you*. But then one day, she asked me to choose. And at the time, she seemed like the more fun, less stressful option."

I step back, baffled at his logic. While I was changing myself, making myself smaller and more palatable to keep the peace between us, he was…*fucking someone else*? And then he chose *her* over me, when I was the one with the ring?

"Why didn't you *tell me* you were struggling so much with all the pressure?" I ask through gritted teeth. "We could have gone to couples counseling."

He scoffs. "And what, have *two* therapy people breathing

down my neck? You're a fucking relationship advice columnist. Do you not realize how intimidating that is? If I told you everything that I was feeling, you'd probably try to therapize me like I'm one of your readers. And then you'd get an actual professional for backup to basically repeat everything you told me."

I briefly close my eyes. Every single one of James's words cuts through my heart like a knife. "You don't know that, and we'll *never* know how I'll really react, because you didn't even try to get help. Also, don't blame me for something *you* did. Cheating to cope with things instead of *talking* is not normal!"

We glare at each other, wide-eyed and red-faced, breathing heavily and our nostrils flaring in the living room where we previously only used to laugh.

"This was a mistake," I say, heading back to the door. "Just donate all my stuff to charity. Or dump it. I don't want any reminders of the time we spent together."

I don't even give him a chance to respond before I leave the condo.

39

Gemma

James's revelation that he cheated pretty much ruins the entire city of San Francisco for me. It was bad enough before, since almost all my memories of this place are with James. But it's way worse now, with the added knowledge that James was sleeping with someone else for who knows how long in our relationship. And he probably went to the same places with her, too.

I love Kiara and Val, but I can't get over the fact that the entire reason why I moved here in the first place was for a job I got with James. I need a big change in my life. Fast. I need to go somewhere else, to live a life that'll make *me* happy.

I don't expect the NYC job to be still available, nor am I really interested in it, but for the next few weeks, I routinely check in with Evelyn to see if there are any other positions

I can apply for. One that's ideally on the West Coast so I'd still be close to my friends and family.

"A job *is* available down in Irvine, in Orange County," Evelyn says one day, making me perk up.

I'm from Irvine, and my parents still live in the house I grew up in. The area is quieter and more suburban than San Francisco, and as a teenager, it seemed like the most boring place on Earth. But now, the very prospect of moving back to my hometown, of being closer to my parents and all the familiar restaurants and stores of my childhood, is comforting.

And thankfully, now that I'm an adult, I can drive up to LA whenever I get sick of suburbia. Or at least, I should be able to, in theory. It's been several years since I last got behind the wheel, but hopefully it'll all come back to me. I'll worry about driving and other logistics later, after I actually get the job.

"Great!" I say excitedly. "I'll apply for the position—"

"This office is more visual media based than text, though," Evelyn cuts in. "So you'll be working as a multimedia journalist, rather than a staff writer. The job doesn't *quite* match your qualifications, but maybe 'Modern Love in Focus' will give you an edge, since you conducted the interviews and Citrine liked it so much. I'll put in a good word."

"That's fine," I say. "Thank you, Evelyn."

"You're very welcome."

Because I don't want to blindside them if I do get the job, I stop by my friends' apartment after work to broach the possibility.

When I finish telling them everything, from my discovery about James to this new job, Kiara and Val stare back at me with wide eyes. They both look devastated for me, and Kiara cries.

Finally, Val says, "I think this move will be great for you. You'll be closer to family, and it'll still be a relatively fresh start, since you haven't lived in the area for, what, more than ten years? You *would* be getting your own place, though, right? Not that there's anything wrong with living with the parents."

I nod. "Oh, definitely. Maybe not right away, since I'll need to save some money first. But this job comes with a pay bump, so I'll eventually be able to move out and get a small studio for myself."

Kiara squeezes my shoulder. "That'd be so amazing, Gemma. Okay, yeah, I approve. Let's manifest this move for you!"

I gratefully squeeze Kiara's hand.

"Besides, Orange County isn't *that* far," Val says. "You'll come visit us, right?"

"Yup, it's not bad at all. I'll still be in California. And of course! We have a wedding to plan! If I do move, *you two* should also visit me in SoCal. We have Disneyland, Joshua Tree, LA, San Diego…oh, and we're closer to Vegas and Mexico!"

Val rubs her hands. "Oh, man, yeah, we'll be visiting all the time after the wedding, then. You're going to get *so* sick of us."

I laugh. "Never! You guys will always be welcome at my place, no matter where I live."

I apply and interview for the position. A few weeks pass without any news, and I'd assumed I didn't get the position when I get a call.

"Gemma?" It's Evelyn.

Since we communicate primarily via email, I know something must be up. I hold my breath as she continues speaking.

"Congratulations," she says. "You got the job."

~

My move to Orange County is as smooth as it can be. Thanks to the onrush of newly minted college graduates looking for jobs in the summer, I manage to find someone to replace me at Ms. Chang's fairly quickly. Of course, I didn't have to, but after all the kindness she and her husband showed me while I lived with them, I didn't want to leave without finding them a replacement.

Like I told my friends I would, I move back in with my parents, who *love* having me around again. Mom and Dad fuss over me like I never left for college. And, unlike when I was younger, I let them, thinking back to how nervous Ms. Chang and her husband were about sending their daughter off to school. Of course, now that my parents are older, I fuss over them, too, helping out around the house whenever I can and making sure they're taking care of *themselves*.

Surprisingly, the most challenging thing about the move is getting a car, which I need right away since my new office is on the opposite side of town from our house. I have to rely on my parents and rideshare apps for the first few weeks, but we finally manage to get a good deal on a used car thanks to a family friend from church. And I still remember how to drive. Somewhat. Obviously, I need a lot of practice to get completely used to maneuvering a car again, but thankfully I can take local roads to get to work.

The Irvine office is slightly bigger than the one in San Francisco and is located in a bungalow built in the typical Southern Californian orange roof and white exterior Spanish villa style, rather than being in an office building in the middle of a city. The staff is bigger, too, covering events, lifestyle, real estate, and entertainment in not just Orange County but also the greater Los Angeles area.

It's my first time fully working with a team to create multimedia content, rather than just writing assignments on my own. It's invigorating and challenging, all at once, and I often find myself working longer, later hours than I ever did in San Francisco because of all the new skills I have to learn on the go. There's a steep learning curve, but I enjoy everything even more than I thought I would.

If I'm being totally honest, though, the best part of my new job is not the work itself. It's the fact that I have higher pay and better health insurance. Which is great because boy, do therapy bills add up, especially when you have a lot to work on like I do.

In November, six months after I moved back in with

my parents, I get a studio apartment for myself in a nearby city that has cheaper rent than Irvine. Even a tiny studio of my own seems like a big upgrade after all the places I've lived in the past year or so. It's my first time having my own place, without any parents, lovers, or roommates... *ever.* And that makes me so happy I don't know what to do with myself.

I manage to get very affordable pieces of furniture from Ikea, even finding a small orange sofa to put at the foot of my bed, in honor of Clementine. As great as Clementine was, this is one couch I hope I'll never have to sleep on.

When I'm finally all moved in, I sit on my bed and take a few quiet deep breaths. Somehow, I made it. I made it out of San Francisco and finally have my own place to call home.

I'm all by myself, but for the first time ever, I'm okay with it. Or at least, I think I'm starting to be.

Celeste

When her agent sends her the first roundup of available jobs in the area for the new year, Celeste doesn't expect to see Gemma's name attached to one of them. But there she is, clear as day, the lead journalist on a project that's vaguely reminiscent of "Modern Love in Focus."

Intrigued, Celeste clicks through to read the description. Unlike the project Celeste worked on with Gemma, this newly proposed one focuses on younger couples and is purely visual media based. And instead of interviewing many different people, it follows two couples over the course of a year, revisiting with them every six months to see how they change—if at all. It's an ambitious project, and one that sounds very cool at that. Celeste feels a rush of pride that Gemma is at the helm of it.

From watching Gemma's Instagram Stories—a guilty pleasure of hers that, to her therapist's chagrin, she could never get rid of no matter how hard she tried—she knows that Gemma relocated to SoCal at some point. She just doesn't know where and why.

Without logging in, Celeste surreptitiously looks at Gemma's thankfully public LinkedIn profile. It says Gemma relocated to Citrine's office in Irvine as a multimedia journalist in May, so eight months ago. A promotion, maybe. But the fact that she suddenly moved to *Irvine*, where her parents live, of all places, concerns Celeste.

Did something happen with her family? Celeste reaches for her phone... and then stops herself. Aside from wishing each other a happy birthday, Celeste to Gemma in March and Gemma to Celeste in June, they haven't interacted with each other at all in the past several months.

A year is nothing compared to the eight they previously spent apart, but for some reason, this period of time has felt a lot longer for Celeste, and somehow more excruciating. It'd gotten to the point that she had to resume therapy, which she'd previously quit a couple of years ago, so she could have someone—other than Min-joon, who has his own drama to deal with these days—to help sort out her thoughts and feelings after what happened between her and Gemma.

Unsurprisingly, her therapist, who for years has been *appalled* by her absolute refusal to engage in romantic relationships, is in good spirits when Celeste updates her about Gemma.

"Maybe you should consider reaching out to her," Dr. Espinosa cheerfully suggests. "Properly this time. If only to check in on her to make sure she's okay. Throw the ball in her court. If she chooses to engage with you, then great. If not, that's great, too. It'll be a sign for you to respectfully move on."

Celeste can't resist joking, "Or I could *not* talk to her and be forever alone."

Her therapist sighs. "Or that. And if that's genuinely what you want, I'd be all for it! I have clients who are aromantic or asexual, and there's nothing wrong with identifying as such. But, Celeste, we both know you're not one of them. I'm not encouraging you to jump into a relationship with your ex. By all means, please *don't*. However, I feel like it'll be good for you to just catch up with Gemma, if she's up for it. She seems special to you in a way that no one else ever was, to the point that you haven't been able to move on from her for almost ten years."

"*Ten?*" Celeste balks, sitting up from her seat.

"Right." Dr. Espinosa checks her notes. "Well, it's more like a little over nine, since it's January, and it was December when you first left Gemma. But I'm rounding up in the spirit of the New Year. And it might get to ten if you let things stay the same from now until December."

Celeste adds "the relentless passage of time" to her list of discussion topics for their next session.

"You deserve happiness, Celeste," her therapist says, firmly but gently. "I know it's scary to go for the things you want, especially after you've grown up in environments that tell you that you don't deserve to live the life you want to live. But isn't it better to be scared and take a shot at happiness, instead of avoiding it all the time?"

Back home at her desk, Celeste stares at the project listing again. After how things ended between them—and how she disappeared from Gemma's life, once again—Celeste has no idea if Gemma even wants to hear from her again. But there's no harm in just talking to her and seeing how she's doing, is there? Especially if something *did* happen to her and her family?

Thinking back to her therapist's advice, Celeste formulates a plan. Rather than send a text that could potentially go embarrassingly unanswered, she'll meet Gemma face-to-face. And what better way to meet Gemma than to apply for this job that she's really interested in?

"Throw the ball in her court," Dr. Espinosa had said.

If no one responds to her application, then that'll be that. Celeste will take it as a sign that Gemma isn't interested in talking with her at all.

Celeste is terrified. But she tells her agent to submit her for the job.

Gemma

I've pretty much settled into my new job *and* my new life when I come across an application with a familiar-looking portfolio on my desk.

"We're currently searching for freelance videographers for the next project we're doing," says Pauline, one of my coworkers. "And this creator comes highly recommended. I think she worked with you on a previous project?"

Celeste's eyes look back at me from the center photo, her expression the perfect mix of wistful and charismatic. Along with her picture are four photos she took, two of which are from our project.

"We also have her video work on file, but I figured you've already seen it, so I didn't bother forwarding that email," Pauline adds when I don't respond right away.

I'm surprised to realize that, with how busy I've been

lately, I haven't thought about Celeste in a while. Despite the quieter pace of life in the suburbs, socially and professionally, I've been busier than ever. I've been dividing my time between helping Kiara and Val plan their wedding, throwing myself into work, and making new—as well as reconnecting with the old—friends here in SoCal. It's been chaotic, but the good kind that helps me fall asleep exhausted every night but wake up feeling rejuvenated and ready to tackle the day in the morning. I can't remember the last time I've been this happy.

But now, with my ex's face right there in front of me, I'm so caught off guard that my voice barely comes out when I say, "We did."

Pauline covers her mouth with her hands. "Oh dear. Did you not like working with her? We can remove her from the list, then, no problem."

Slowly, I trace Celeste's photo with my fingers. I take a breath, and then another, trying to gauge how I feel about her now that the initial shock is fading away.

"No," I finally say. "Let's bring her in and see what she has to say. She's one of the best media artists I know. We probably won't find a better person for the job."

We schedule a meeting with Celeste for the following Monday. Technically, meetings with freelancers are done in the conference room with the whole team, but I tell everyone that I'd like to handle this one on my own. And my coworkers are all busy enough with other projects that they're more than happy to let me take charge.

After how emotional things were the last time we saw each other, I have no idea how things will be when we meet again. So I can't help but tense up a bit when she enters the conference room—early, of course. Her hair is longer, flowing gracefully down her back like a silky black waterfall. But other than that, she looks the same. Still unforgettably hot and irritatingly sexy.

As she takes a seat across the table from me, she looks around, her eyebrows lifting as she takes in the sleek interior of the conference room. But then her gaze lands on me, and her eyes soften with an all-too-familiar tenderness that makes my heart skip a beat.

I take a deep breath and lean forward, facing her. "Hi," I say. "First things first...how did you even know that I work here? Are you actually interested in this job?"

Celeste blinks. "Oh, I definitely am. It sounds cool, and I'm not saying that for the hell of it. But I'm also here for you, Gem."

Gem. The familiarity of the nickname almost makes me tear up. "How so?"

She nervously bites her lip before continuing, "I saw that you moved back to Irvine last year. And I was worried that something happened, with you or your family. Going back to your hometown after *twelve* years? That's a pretty big change. It reminded me of what I had to do in college, and I wanted to check in to see if everything was okay."

"Oh." I sit back in my chair. I was expecting a lot of different things, but Celeste popping back into my life because she was *worried* about me wasn't one of them. My heart flutters again, and I feel like I'm about to cry again. Not because I'm sad, but quite the opposite.

Tears escape from my eyes, and almost immediately, Celeste comes over to give me a hug.

"Oh, no, Gemma baby," she says. "Is everyone okay? I'm so sorry—"

I wave my hands in front of me before she can continue. "No, sorry." I'm freely crying now, but I'm smiling, too. "Everyone's fine. I'm sorry I made you worry. Thank you, really. But no. I just needed to get out of San Francisco. And I got this new, higher-paying position close to home, so."

"Wait," Celeste says, cocking her head to the side. "But then why are you crying?"

My cheeks heat up in embarrassment. "Oh, I'm . . . happy. Life's been so good since I moved back to SoCal. And now you're here in front of me, saying you applied for a job because you're *worried* about me? I feel so blessed."

Celeste's face softens, her shoulders finally relaxing as she smiles. "I'm glad to hear that. You deserve nothing but the best."

My heart's beating loudly in my chest now, irrepressible and undeniable. "Thank you, Celeste. Really."

She peers at me from under those damn long lashes of hers. We stay there like that for one long moment, inches away from one another.

She clears her throat. "Okay, well, since everything is okay, I also wanted to talk to you about something else."

I frown. "About what?"

"I..." Celeste trails off and looks away from me. She starts to say something, pauses again, and then finally goes on. "I think I overreacted. Back when we were in SF. There was a lot going on, and I was super overwhelmed, even more than I realized at the time. Yes, some time apart was good for us, and I don't regret that part, especially after seeing how *happy* you are now. But I didn't need to completely disappear from your life again, and I'm sorry. I regretted it a lot over the past year, to the point that I'm sure my therapist is sick of me talking about you."

"Wait, you're in therapy?" I ask, since I'm still wrapping my mind around everything else she just said. "I am, too!"

Celeste's eyebrows shoot up in confusion. It's probably not something to be super happy about, but after all the drama that went down with James admitting he chose to cheat on me instead of going to couples counseling, I can't help but feel relieved. My advice columnist days are long gone, but I'm so glad Celeste and I are *actually* working on ourselves.

When I don't say anything else out loud, Celeste's expression deepens into a frown. "Wait, you didn't go to therapy because of me, did you?"

"Kind of?" I admit honestly. "But also, not really. What you said about me, about how I kept jumping from relationship to relationship... it made me realize I had a dependency problem. So I've been working on that. *And* staying single for the past year. It's been helping a lot."

A huge smile blooms across Celeste's face. She looks so genuinely happy for me that I smile, too. "That's great to hear, Gem. I'm proud of you."

Suddenly, she lets out a dry laugh. "My mistake was ever thinking I could do anything casual with you. Did you know it's been over nine years since we first broke up? That's almost a decade! And yet I'm still as obsessed with you now as I was then. I should have told you that instead of saying whatever the fuck I did back in SF."

My heart's pounding so loudly that I can barely hear my own voice. "Are you saying what I think you're saying?"

Celeste bites her lip and nods. "I'd understand if you're not up for it, because God knows you already gave me enough chances. But I want to try seriously dating you again, Gem. We don't have to jump into a relationship right away, especially not since you've been enjoying being single so much. We can go as slow as you want, maybe go thirty-five miles per hour instead of doing a hundred twenty. Whatever you're comfortable with. I don't care as long as we do things properly this time."

I laugh at Celeste's random driving metaphor. It's funny, but effective, since I know exactly what she's talking about.

"To be fair, we had absolutely no chance of going at a normal speed from the very beginning," I reply. "Since we started off as roommates."

Celeste's eyes widen with realization. "You're absolutely right," she says with a groan. "And they were roommates! Ironically that's one of my favorite romantic tropes."

"Jeez, I wonder why." I snicker, and so does she.

When we've grown serious again, I say exactly what I want to Celeste. I don't dance around things, nor do I say what I think she'd want to hear. "I want to try again, too. Just slowly, like you said. But also—and sorry, I'm not trying to be mean here—I thought you don't do relationships, Celeste. I get that you still have feelings for me, but why did that change?"

She shrugs. "My therapist said this thing. She told me that just because I'm scared shitless, doesn't mean I shouldn't try something. Well, I'm paraphrasing, but yeah. And it made me realize that, even though I'm terrified and may still have a lot to work on before I feel completely ready, I do want to try everything with you, Gem. I want a shot at our happily-ever-after."

I kiss her, unable to resist any longer.

"You don't have to be perfect," I say, resting the tip of my nose on hers. "No one is. We all have our faults, and we all have our own baggage. You don't have to be this flawless goddess to date me. I've always just wanted *you*."

Celeste nods. Her voice comes out raw, sounding more vulnerable than I've ever heard it before when she says, "I've always just wanted you, too. I don't want to share my life with anyone else."

My vision goes blurry with tears. "Same here."

She stares at me for one long moment. Then, a mischievous quirk appears on her lips. "So, does that mean I got the job?"

I smile and pull her in for another kiss.

Epilogue

Celeste and I don't move in together right away. We don't even start staying overnight at each other's places until a full month after we start dating again, and only when we feel absolutely ready. Even then, we keep things separate, only seeing each other when we need to for work and on weekends—but not *every* weekend.

The U-Haul lesbian life may work for some people, but we need more time and space. For now, anyway. And it's nice. I'm still enjoying living alone. But I'm also enjoying my time with Celeste.

In lieu of living together, we go on a lot of dates, and do short little trips in-state. And that's exactly what we do one weekend in the spring, with Celeste tagging along when I return to San Francisco to help with last-minute preparations for Kiara and Val's wedding.

When we're all done with errands for the big day, my

friends and I meet up at the gorgeous Palace of Fine Arts. Kiara and Val are getting *married* here tomorrow. My skin buzzes with excitement at the thought.

Despite its name, the Palace is more of a huge, Greco-Roman rotunda with beautiful green lawns and a lagoon. Over a hundred feet tall and surrounded by ancient-looking columns, the entire area is picturesque and mystical, practically glowing in the afternoon light. The perfect setting for a very sapphic wedding.

"I know it's too late to make changes now, the day before the wedding," Kiara says when we meet up in the parking lot. "But I wanted to chill here for a bit to make sure the vibes are right. Plus, I figured it'd be nice for us to hang out, since I doubt we'll have time to talk much tomorrow."

"It was a great call," I agree. "Coming to the venue in a much more casual context can also help with your nerves."

My friends laugh at what I said, and I smile sheepishly when I realize I slipped into my advice columnist past self without even realizing it.

"It's nice to meet you properly as Gemma's girlfriend," Val says, reaching around me and Kiara to give Celeste a firm handshake. "With all your clothes on."

I laugh the hardest this time, and Celeste blushes as Kiara also shakes her hand. "Pleasure to meet you, Celeste," she says.

"It's nice to meet you both," Celeste replies. "Congratulations. I'm looking forward to the wedding."

Collectively, the four of us have filled our picnic baskets to the brim with various cheeses, jams, crackers, wines, and salami. We went a bit overboard, and at least two wine bottles stick out from the baskets.

Val lays out a large checkered blanket for us to sit on and passes out wineglasses. Kiara and I take out the food and arrange it on our charcuterie board as aesthetically pleasingly as we can. Before we dig in, Celeste takes a few pictures, of our food, the Palace, and of us, with her professional camera.

"We make an amazing team," Kiara says. "And we're so lucky to have you two to help out with the wedding. More double dates like this, *please*!"

"You guys should come down to SoCal next time," I reply. "Now that you'll be done with all the wedding craziness. You'll love Balboa Park, Kiara. It's an hour and a half from where I live, but Celeste and I can drive down and meet you guys there. It's a similar vibe to this, but bigger."

"That's in San Diego, right?" Val asks. "Our wallets will need to recover first but, afterward, yeah, we'll be there!"

Couples of all different races, genders, and sexualities picnic around us, and along with the idyllic, peaceful atmosphere created by the beautiful scenery, I've never felt safer. Val and Kiara must feel the same, because, after a while, their shoulders relax and they stare lovingly into each other's eyes.

Celeste, too, seems to be enjoying herself. And her face is full of wonder and awe at our surroundings as she sips her wine.

"I can't believe a place like this *exists*," she says after we finish eating. "Like, I drove by it a couple of times when I was visiting the city for work, but I thought it was just some big monument or something."

"Isn't it amazing?" I say. "Totally random, but cool. As for me, *I* can't believe I'm here with all of you guys. Like, I'm so happy right now!"

I give Celeste a light peck on her lips before throwing out my arms to my sides to hug Val and Kiara. "You guys are getting *married*! How are you feeling?"

My friends look at each other again.

"Honestly, I was a nervous wreck before you came," Kiara says. "So I'm so glad you and Celeste are here with us."

"Same here," Val adds with wide eyes. "Really, even this picnic is helping a lot."

"I'm glad we could help," I say. "I wouldn't miss this for the world."

"Aw, Gemma!" Kiara exclaims. "We love you so much!"

Val nods in agreement, and we all come together for a big hug.

After we say goodbye to my friends, Celeste drives us over to the Golden Gate Park. It's only six minutes away, and the weather's perfect for a little stroll.

"I remember being so pissed off when I found out that this park isn't next to the bridge," Celeste muses when we get out of her car.

"Ah yeah," I laugh. "It's named after the Golden Gate strait. Just Gold Rush things, you know?"

What's nice about the Golden Gate Park is that, unlike many other urban parks, it's relatively removed from downtown. Stepping into its grounds makes it feel like we're transported to another world. A family of bikers rides past us, laughing and chatting, and tourists take group selfies at the flower beds in full bloom as we walk by them.

Celeste and I end up going around the park until sunset. The lake shimmers in the fading sunlight, and the sky is a gorgeous purple and pink. We've been in a comfortable silence for a while now, and I turn around to see that she's staring at me, her eyes dark and thoughtful.

"Gem," she says when our eyes meet. "I was waiting for the right moment to say this, since the last time I said these three words, it was . . . in not ideal circumstances. But I love you. A lot."

I feel the same way and have for a while now. But after what happened the last time we said we love each other, I can't help but feel a little nervous. Although things have been *so* good ever since we decided to try dating again, there's still a small part of me that's afraid she might change her mind and leave again.

Something in my eyes must have revealed all the different emotions going through my head, because Celeste closes the distance between us. Before I know it, we're kissing, her soft lips pressed against mine and our tongues saying the things we can't.

"I love you, too," I say, finally building up enough courage to do it.

Celeste beams. Then she suddenly laughs.

"What?" I ask, still smiling but a bit confused.

"Sorry," Celeste says. "It occurred to me that this exact moment, us kissing in a romantic park during sunset... it's a total romance book moment."

"You and those romance books," I tease. "Are there any other romance novel moments you've always wanted to try out in real life?"

"Getting married," she says, so quickly that I gasp in surprise. "But I don't think we're quite there yet. I still have days when I'm convinced a happy marriage is a total myth. For people like me, I mean. Not for Kayla or your friends."

I groan. "Well, it's a good thing we don't plan on getting married anytime soon. Anything else?"

"Cute picnic dates at the park." She gives me a small, shy smile.

I laugh. "Check."

She nods. "Thanks to Val and Kiara. Speaking of, I've also always wanted to attend a wedding with a partner. Since that's a common romance book activity."

I nod. "Well, keep hitting me with more of your romance novel bucket list ideas. We might be able to work our way up to marriage after all."

"Maybe so." Celeste gives my hand a light squeeze. "If I do end up getting married, there's no one else I'd rather do it with than you."

I squeeze her hand back. "I feel the same way about you."

We stay like that for a long time, looking into each other's eyes.

"Like you said, one step at a time," Celeste says. "Or I guess, one romance novel moment at a time?"

"I like that. One romance novel moment at a time."

Later that evening, we're walking back to our hotel when Celeste says, "So, I don't know about you, but I could use some shaved ice. No worries if you're too full from dinner, though."

I lightly slap her arm. "Of course not! What kind of Korean would I be if I didn't have room for *bingsu*?"

She chuckles. "All right then, we could go to the place we went to last time. *Or*, there's another Asian dessert café on Sixteenth Street that I heard was good."

"Let's try the new place," I say almost immediately. "I may be a long-term relationship girlie, but that doesn't mean I'm not a ho when it comes to dessert."

Celeste laughs and wraps her arm around my shoulders as we head back toward her car.

"I'm so excited for all the dessert places we'll explore together, Gem," she says, suddenly growing serious. "And for all the romance book memories we'll make together."

"Me, too."

She pulls me into a kiss that's not quite as sweet as ice cream but is pretty damn close.

Acknowledgments

First and foremost, thank you, reader, for picking up this book. Getting published as a person of color is difficult in the US, but it's even more so difficult when you're also queer and want to tell queer love stories. It took me a while to be able to write this story, and I appreciate you for taking a chance on it.

Next, I would like to thank my literary agent, Penny Moore, who never once batted an eyelash when I told her I wanted to try my hand at writing romance books, my favorite genre as a reader myself. Thank you always for your astute insights and incredible business acumen and for that one fateful day when you said, "Hey, how about you try this?" This book wouldn't exist without you. Thank you also to my editor, Junessa Viloria, and the rest of my incredibly passionate and wonderful team at Forever. Thank you, everyone, for the long hours and for the countless emails. We all deserve a break after this.

I would also like to thank SASS (the Subtle Asian Sapphic Squad), for being the international sapphic community

I never thought I'd be able to find when I was a questioning and closeted teen growing up in a highly traditional Korean immigrant household in Texas. I'm so lucky that I found y'all, and I get so happy just *thinking* about the group's existence. Thank you to all the friends I met, online and in real life, through SASS. I wrote this book for us.

Last but not least, I need a whole separate section to thank the incredible artists whose musical masterpieces filled with *sapphic yearning* are the beating heart of this book. I doubt any of them will ever read this, but I'm literally listening to "Good Luck, Babe!" as I write this, so might as well! Of course, thank you, Chappell Roan, for *The Rise and Fall of a Midwest Princess*. Seriously, so good, no skips. I listened to the album on repeat while working on this book, and all the songs are relevant to this book in some way. And thank you to my all-time fave, Halsey, whose duet with Lauren Jauregui, "Strangers," lived rent-free in my head for *years* before I ever thought of writing this book. I also definitely can't forget to thank Hayley Kiyoko, our Lesbian Jesus, for giving Asian sapphics like me the pop-cultural representation we've always wanted. Finally, thank you, FLETCHER for "girls girls girls" and Billie Eilish for the incredible sonic and emotional journey that is the album *Hit Me Hard and Soft*. Wow, I love women.

About the Author

Lyla Lee is the bestselling author of *Love in Focus, The Cuffing Game*, and other swoony rom-com books inspired by pop culture and her Korean heritage. Her books have been translated into multiple languages around the world. Originally from South Korea, she's lived in various cities throughout the United States, worked various jobs in Hollywood, and studied psychology and cinematic arts at the University of Southern California. She now lives in Dallas, Texas.

To learn more, visit her at:

lylaleebooks.com
Facebook.com/authorlylalee
Instagram @authorlylalee
TikTok @authorlylalee